THE
MISFIT
MISSION

More praise for *The Misfit Mission*

"Scott Chrostek has long been the most interesting pastor you've not yet heard of. With this book the world will know what a gifted storyteller, what a brilliant mind, what a radiant heart he is. Fear not, church. God is raising up the leaders we need. Here's one. Take up and read."
–Jason Byassee, Butler Chair of Preaching, Vancouver School of Theology

"I am a bishop of The United Methodist Church and one of God's Misfits. In this book, Scott Chrostek helps me see God's work clearly and how my discipleship fits into a larger picture of how God uses everyone for God's mission. This is a book that greatly helps us in our discipleship journey."
–Scott J. Jones, Bishop, Great Plains Conference (UMC)

"If you or your church happens to be in need of a big dose of *hope*, read this book! With compelling stories and convincing insights Scott shares the 'why to' and the 'how to' of witnessing to the power of God in a way that can reach any person and transform any church."
–Jim Ozier, New Church Development & Congregational Transformation, North Texas Conference, United Methodist Church

THE

how to change the world

MISFIT

with surprises, interruptions,

MISSION

and all the wrong people

Scott Chrostek

 Abingdon Press™

Nashville

THE MISFIT MISSION:
HOW TO CHANGE THE WORLD WITH SURPRISES,
INTERRUPTIONS, AND ALL THE WRONG PEOPLE

Library of Congress Cataloging-in-Publication Data has been requested.

ISBN 978-1-5018-0608-7

16 17 18 19 20 21 22 23 24 25—10 9 8 7 6 5 4 3 2 1
MANUFACTURED IN THE UNITED STATES OF AMERICA

CONTENTS

THE MISFIT MISSION: A JOURNEY OF HOLY SURPRISE

Whenever God wants to do something extraordinary, God almost always uses the wrong people. God is the God of great surprises and holy reversals. There's the unexpected choice, the unconventional way, and the unpredictable outcome. This is God's way. As an adolescent, I remember being forced to read Charles Dickens's *Great Expectations*. It actually became one of my favorite books, yet I've come to discover that with God there are no great expectations. God favors the unexpected. If God's story were a novel, it would be entitled *Great Unexpectations* because God's story is a story that always involves the wrong people, the unlikely candidates, or the ill-equipped persons of this world. This is what resides at the heart of God's Misfit Mission.

God calls and invites each of us into life-giving and world-changing mission in spite of who we are. These pages are filled with a collection of stories and insights about life, work, and God's Misfit Mission (the holy adventure unto which we are all called). A lot of the stories contained within these pages stem from my personal experience as pastor of Resurrection Downtown, a fledgling church in downtown Kansas City, Missouri. In its first five years Resurrection Downtown has grown from a handful of individuals (nine of us) into a community that worships with more than one thousand adults on a weekly basis.

Through my journey launching Resurrection Downtown, I have experienced a pattern of wrong decisions, wrong people, wrong places, and wrong times. Every step of the journey has been filled with holy surprises and unexpected people or what I now call God's Misfits. Yet, after six years, we have become a community rooted in God's call and our unwavering commitment to respond to that call by doing what almost always appears to be "the wrong things." Yet, these "wrong things" have somehow become increasingly "right" in light of God's Misfit Mission. We've hired the wrong people. We've moved into the wrong buildings. We've worshipped at the wrong times. We started with the wrong number of people who were from the wrong end of the spectrum. Nothing has fit together. If you can name it, we have done it the wrong way, which is ultimately God's way, God's Misfit Way.

Through our community's willingness to respond to God's call, God has made possible a story of numerical growth and communal transformation both within the church and throughout the city. By sharing bits and pieces of the RezDowntown story, I hope that both you and your congregations will be challenged and encouraged to think creatively about how God *might be calling you* to transform the world around you through bold and courageous leadership rooted in God's perfect love. I pray that this book may inspire you to become the best version of the people, leaders, or communities that God has created you to be, namely capable of abundantly far more than anything you could ever think to ask or imagine (cf. Eph 3:20).

Before we begin, here are a couple of working definitions to help shape your reading of this book. The first term we need to understand is what I mean by a misfit.

The Misfit: A misfit is a person called by God, generally understood by society or the culture at large to be the unlikely candidate, a poor fit, the long shot, or a holy surprise. A misfit can be woefully underqualified or perhaps overqualified. A misfit can be too old or too young, but is often not the right age. A misfit is either too experienced or not experienced enough. He or she is either well before his or her prime or well past it. A misfit can be considered to be the least, the lost, marginalized, oppressed, forgotten, or pigeonholed. Misfits are people who have been created by God with a capacity to reflect God's image and an ability to do the things that God does. Misfits are God's craftsmanship, created beings ripe with God's creative possibilities to accomplish abundantly far more than anything we could think to ask or imagine. We are all misfits, regardless of our age, stage, occupation, status, power, or persuasion.

The Mission: The mission is to employ the gifts that God has given you to the extent that you are able to transform the world by doing the things that God does—by living, loving, and letting your light so shine before others to the extent that others will see the work you do and give glory to God in heaven, until we all experience thy kingdom come, together, here on earth just as it is in heaven.

Who are you?

Are you a student wondering what God is calling you to do with your life?

Are you at a crossroads in your professional life, wondering what you should do or become in order to make the most impact?

Are you approaching retirement age, uncertain of what the future holds and what you will do with all of your newly found free time?

Are you a stay-at-home mom looking for meaning, purpose, and value beyond the full-time job you currently hold as COO of your family's household?

Are you feeling stuck at work and looking for hope, or are you a pastor feeling stuck in ministry wondering what God has done by placing you in your current appointment or ministry context?

Is your ministry team wondering what God might be calling you to do in order to accomplish abundantly far more than you could ask or imagine?

Do any of these questions apply to you?
If so, then you might be one of God's Misfits.
Regardless of who you are or where you're from, God is calling you and has equipped you with the ability to change the world. I hope you will encounter the Living God through reading this book, and I hope that in meeting

God or hearing God's call you will be inspired, renewed, and emboldened to go forth as one of God's Misfits called into mission.

May God fill you with grace and peace as together we seek to do the things God does, perhaps even greater things this day and every day.

CHAPTER ONE

GOD'S WRONG WAY: GOD CHOOSES US FIRST

When it comes to looking for a way forward, we almost always look to experts for advice. We read bestsellers, attend leadership conferences, visit with life coaches, or invest our money in endless personality tests and strength finders.

What would happen if we looked for help elsewhere?

What if we looked to scripture instead?

What if we didn't focus first on the well-known or venerated but instead immersed ourselves in the volumes of scripture filled with stories about the immeasurable and unpredictable God of the universe?

If you turn through the pages of scripture, you'll uncover one of the most formative, encouraging, and perhaps surprising lessons on leadership ever. In John 14:12, Jesus says,

> I assure you that whoever believes in me will do the works that I do. They will do even greater works than these because I am going to the Father.

No matter how imperfect or fallible we might feel from time to time, God has created us with a capacity to do the things that God does and, in fact, greater things. This is extraordinary.

Do you feel as though you are doing the things that God does?

Are you doing greater things?

Do you believe you can?

In John 14, Jesus assures us of our capacity to change the world, and then he encourages us to go to work believing this to be true.

In his letter to the Ephesians, the Apostle Paul wrote to his community from a dark, dank, unsanitary prison. As he addressed his church in Ephesus, he offered them (and us) a similar lesson on leadership. Paul wrote of God's immeasurable and unpredictable power, saying,

> Glory to God, who is able to do far beyond all that we could ask or imagine by his power at work within us. (Eph 3:20)

In confinement, Paul reminded his congregation that no matter how dark, dank, or unsanitary things become, even if you find yourself in prison, by God's grace we have the power to change the world. It doesn't matter how stuck, how inadequate, or how hopeless you feel; by the power of God's grace we are able to accomplish the extraordinary (far beyond all that you could ask or imagine).

Do you feel stuck?

Are you without hope?

Are you sitting at a crossroads?

Do you believe that you are able to accomplish far beyond all that we could ask or imagine?

Paul encourages us from prison, sitting shackled in darkness, to believe this. At a time when the whole Roman world would have written Paul off, the Apostle Paul pressed on. Paul had the strength to encourage others always, saying,

> Even when you are imprisoned like me, shackled by chains, God is able to use you, work through you, maybe even in spite of you to accomplish the extraordinary. Through Christ all things possible.

This is God's call and scriptural promise to us. We are capable of surpassing expectations. We are capable of surprising the status quo. We are created and gifted with a capacity to do the things that God does, even greater things. We are filled with the grace of Jesus Christ that allows us to accomplish far beyond all that we could ask or imagine.

Scripture reaffirms this time and time again. All throughout the Bible you'll find story after story of God calling ordinary people to do extraordinary things, and they actually do them. In the process they become God's Misfits in Mission.

In Exodus, God called Moses (a murderer) to lead the Israelites out of Egyptian slavery. God's Misfit. In Jeremiah, God called Jeremiah (a boy) to pluck up and tear down, to plant and overthrow. God's Misfit. In the Gospels, the angel of the Lord informed Mary (a young, unwed virgin) that she was going to conceive and bear a child who will be the Messiah, the Lord. God's Misfit. In each of these accounts,

3

God called unlikely candidates, and upon doing so, God reminded and assured them saying, "You didn't choose me, but I chose you" (John 15:16). And then they responded by living fully into the future without fear, trusting in the validity of God's call or invitation.

After reading through the pages of scripture, one thing becomes abundantly clear. It doesn't matter who you are or where you've been because at the heart of God's story is the simple fact that *God chooses us first.*

God invites us. God stirs a passion within our ill-equipped and misfit hearts, and then God equips us with the surprising ability to build Christian community or change the world. This is God's Misfit Mission. This is what God does. God calls the unexpected in the presence of the perceivably predictable to do extraordinary things.

In the Beginning of RezDowntown

In July 2009, my wife and I had been in the ministry for about three years. We were serving two separate churches in Michigan and things were going predictably smooth, and then we found ourselves standing on the precipice of a pretty big and nonsensical opportunity, which in hindsight would become our own Misfit Mission. We received a call to consider making a change of pastoral appointment and were asked whether we would be interested in starting a church in downtown Kansas City, Missouri.

This opportunity didn't fit our experience, qualifications, family history, or current skill set. To say that starting a church in Kansas City was far out of *our* comfort zones would have been an understatement. People from Detroit don't leave home. That wasn't an option for us. Besides being born and raised in the Motor City, Wendy and I had never set foot in Kansas City, and yet as we prayed, we remembered that this is exactly the kind of thing that God does. Whenever God is going to do something extraordinary, God is going to call the wrong people in the wrong places to do the wrong things. God is a God of the holy surprises and epic reversals. This was God calling, the same way God had called both Wendy and me years earlier. I left a career in finance for a life in church. Wendy passed on a future in medicine for a career in ministry. So, once we got past the initial shock of this Kansas City call through prayer and reflection, we began to believe that this was actually God's invitation to become a part of a new and crazy adventure, our very own Misfit Mission.

It took about three months of personal deliberation and denominational delay before we boxed up our stuff, packed the moving van, and transported our entire lives to Kansas City. We arrived on the hottest day of the year: 109 degrees. And let me tell you that we were melting. As we sat outside resting between trips with boxes, we dripped with both sweat and doubt. I suppose you could have called it buyer's remorse, or holy reluctance. In any event, there we sat knowing full well that God called us, we had responded to God's invitation, and there was no going back now. It was terrifying. Like Paul, I like to imagine that we pressed on in fear and trembling.

Within the first week of moving, we quickly realized some limiting factors. One factor was we didn't have any history in our new city. We didn't know anything about Kansas

City or the states of Kansas or Missouri for that matter. We had originally assumed Kansas City was located in Kansas, only to quickly discover that Kansas City is actually located in Missouri. Did you know that?

Another limiting factor was we didn't have any friends. We had no acquaintances to mention. We moved to Kansas City without a network, without knowing the names of anyone, anything, or any street. Needless to say, the only thing we had to hold onto was God's call and each other. We knew God was calling us to do this work, but we didn't feel like we fit the job at hand. We were literally *mis-fits* in *Missouri*. But this is God's recipe, God's Misfit Way.

Whenever God is going to accomplish the extraordinary, God will almost always call the wrong people to do the work. God doesn't opt for the qualified. God doesn't choose the proven. God doesn't call the expected and experienced. God calls misfits. God equips the called, the unlikely candidates, the holy surprises, and the unexpected persons of this world. God chooses us first, regardless of our fitness.

Two fundamental truths about God's Misfit Mission are that

1. God doesn't call the equipped. God equips the called.

2. The people whom God calls are almost always the wrong people for the job.

This was all Wendy and I had to go with upon moving downtown. We were God's misfit candidates called into the mission of building Christian community and transforming the world around us. All we could do was trust that God would make good on God's promise, namely, that we would be equipped with the ability to accomplish the unimaginable task at hand. This was the beginning of our Misfit Mission, and this is the beginning of any Misfit Mission. It is terrifying, uncomfortable, and almost always unexpected. God chooses us first, which is good news, but it should also make you little sick to your stomach.

What is God calling you to do?

What vision for your life, your community, or your church makes you feel both excited and terrified at the same time?

Five years have passed since our move to KC on that hot, fateful day. In that time, Resurrection Downtown has grown from a collection of nine individuals into a community of over one thousand weekly worshippers. As a community, we have endured sanctuaries with one hundred degree heat, malfunctioning bathrooms, limited parking options, and bad sightlines. We have hosted infants' and children's ministries on the floors of free medical clinics mere moments after sweeping up syringes, pills, and medical refuse in scary basements. When we finally did purchase our first space, we chose to purchase and renovate a converted bar/concert venue located next to strip clubs and tattoo parlors. We currently share a parking lot with a pet-delivery business, and we host community dinners in back alleys quite regularly.

Nothing about what we have done or experienced in the past five years has ever made sense to outside observers. You won't find mention of our church in *The Expert's Guide to New Church Starts*, and yet we've experienced exponential growth. But no matter how much growth we have experienced (and hopefully will continue to experience), one common theme has run throughout it all: everything began with God's solitary call. God called two reluctant misfits to move from Detroit to Kansas City. This is God's Misfit Way. God connects the disconnected. God does whatever it takes to find a way forward to accomplish amazing things. And in order to do so, God almost always uses nonsensical people (misfits).

This same pattern can be seen in the archetypal stories of heroes like Abraham, Sarah, Isaac, Jacob, Jonah, Job, Rahab, and David, to name a few. The solitary call of misfit individuals leads to community transformation in ways that far surpass anything we could ask or imagine. We witness the same thing throughout the Gospels as well, in Jesus's mission and ministry through the people he met, healed, led, and redeemed. We see God's Misfit Mission lived out through the Acts of the Apostles, at Pentecost, and through Paul's Epistles to the earliest faith communities, all called to transform the world as God's Misfits in Mission. One can even see God's misfit pattern through the life of Christ. Jesus was the biggest misfit of all.

Jesus was unexpected, unlikely, unsuspecting, and the most undesirable way forward in terms of whom the people imagined the Messiah would be. Jesus was the wrong kind of savior; a Misfit King, to say the least. The scribes and Pharisees longed for a strong and mighty arm, a powerful ruler or a notorious leader with obvious capabilities to overthrow and violently overthrow the Romans. They wanted someone who could throw off the Roman yoke. Instead of meeting their expectations, God surprised them by sending a helpless baby wrapped in swaddling cloths.

Jesus didn't fit in any better when he got older either. In his twenties and thirties, Jesus wasn't anything special. He wasn't the person who most people would have imagined when they dreamt of a world without the Romans or the religious rulers of their day. He was simply the son of carpenter. Jesus came into the world at the **wrong time** (under the cover of night).

Jesus came into the world in the **wrong way** (in a feeding trough).

Jesus came into the world with the **wrong people** (a carpenter and his fourteen-year-old fiancée).

Jesus came into the world with the **wrong words** (bless those who persecute you and love your enemies [Matt 5:44]).

Jesus was the unlikely, the unexpected, and the undesired. Jesus was a misfit, ill-equipped to redeem, reconcile, and restore the world. And yet Jesus was absolutely and unarguably right. This is God's surprising pathway toward life abundant. In God's Misfit Mission, the wrong ones, people like Jesus, are almost always the right people to lead us forward into a future filled with hope. This is the beginning of every great adventure and the pathway toward the life that really is life.

On our first Sunday in Kansas City, before Resurrection Downtown had formed, I had the privilege of attending a worship service at another church. When I arrived at the church, I planned to fly beneath the radar and worship inconspicuously. I wanted to avoid the first-time visitor experience altogether. However, I wanted to know what worship was like at other area churches, so after the worship service concluded I couldn't help but gravitate toward the free coffee. While there, someone engaged me in conversation.

During that conversation I managed to share how I had just moved downtown, and without blinking, my conversation partner left to grab a friend of his, whom he assured me I had to meet.

Anxious and afraid, I clutched my coffee and wondered, "Who does he think that I need to meet?"

Within moments my conversation partner had returned with a woman who looked to be in her forties. He said, "I want you to meet my friend Bobbi Jo. She was a prostitute and lives in your neighborhood. She runs a house full of women in the northeast part of town."

I tried to take in what he was saying without looking shocked, but I was totally confused. Nevertheless, I reached out my hand and said, "Bobbi Jo, I'm pleased to meet you. My name is Scott!"

After the initial shock of his introduction wore off, I had the privilege of learning Bobbi Jo's story. First, she clarified that she used to be a prostitute a long time ago and that she now runs a house (actually a series of houses) for people in recovery... and then she shared her whole story with me.

Bobbi Jo had her first drink at the age of twelve. She drank because her dad was never home and her mom, who was at home, neglected her because of a greater love—prescription pills. She shared how she once accepted an invitation from a couple of older boys, who gave her a taste of beer. That taste quickly turned into alcoholism that then, like her mother, moved into prescription pills. Those pills turned into dealing and then dependency to the point of prostitution.

In her book *Beautifully Broken*, Bobbi Jo writes,

> Sometimes my real introduction gets boiled down to a bunch of
> horrific facts about my life: 24 broken bones, 16 rapes I can re-

member not counting the times I spent as a prostitute or imprisoned as a sex slave, 2 abortions, 1 stint of homelessness, sleeping on an asphalt parking lot under a semi-trailer.[1]

During the worst season of her addiction, something happened to Bobbi Jo. Her dad passed away and that prompted Bobbi Jo to fall to her knees in prayer, confession, and worship. A few months later, her mother lost a battle with cancer, which meant that Bobbi Jo was now the unlikely recipient of an inheritance. Upon receiving this great gift, Bobbi Jo feared that she might slip back into her addiction, given her renewed source of financial security. However, in the wake of her mother's death and in light of her financial gain, she fell to her knees a second time and begged for God's guidance. That's when she heard God's call.

Bobbi Jo heard God calling her to do something extraordinary. God was calling her to care for women who were just like her, those enduring the shackles of addiction and prostitution, in order that they might experience life. So Bobbi Jo purchased an old nursing home, which she restored with her own two hands. In the twelve years since hearing God's calling, Bobbi Jo's nursing home has transformed into a Christian community called the Healing House, which consists of a network of ten houses that serve over one hundred men, women, and children—all of whom are in various stages of recovery after leaving prison, prostitution, addictions, or other circumstances that caused them to feel shame and isolation. Bobbi Jo is literally changing the world by the grace of Jesus Christ. She is a Misfit in Mission.

The Healing House is a thriving community that is changing the world one house and one person at a time. It has grown exponentially in ways that have permanently changed the face of its community, and yet it all began with God's solitary call. God chose Bobbi Jo, a down-on-her-luck addict, and by God's grace she (the wrong person by all accounts) was bold enough to respond. The result was that she accomplished far beyond all that she could ever ask or even imagine. She has changed the world.

In John 15:16, Jesus reminds his disciples and us,

> You didn't choose me, but I chose you and appointed you so that you could go and produce fruit and so that your fruit could last.

God chooses us first. God invites people who are woefully ill-equipped for the task at hand and appoints us in mission to do the things that God does: to bear fruit, fruit that will last. God conscripts all the wrong people to live their lives out loud in response by simply doing the things that God does—maybe even greater things.

God's Misfit Mission begins with the shared understanding that the wrong people are almost always the right ones to carry out God's mission of changing the world. Jesus, who is the foolishness of the cross and the greatest misfit of us all, leads the way forward on our surprising journey filled with God's great un-expectations.

God creates us with a capacity to change the world, and Jesus expects us to live into our capacity by inviting and equipping us to do the things that he does. The Apostle Paul promises us that we can, by the grace of Jesus Christ, accomplish things far greater than anything we could ask or imagine. Time and time again we read stories where God has called and equipped archetypal misfits, people like Abraham, Moses, Jonah, Mary, Rahab, and a bunch of fisherman. God called me, a guy from Detroit, to start a church in Kansas City. God called my friend, Bobbi Jo. Does it make sense to think that God might be calling you, too?

Discussion Questions:

1. Read and recount Moses's call story in Exodus 3:1-12, where God called Moses out of the comfort of Midian and back to Pharaoh on an uncertain holy adventure lacking any comfort at all. Upon reflection, where are you most comfortable? What place of discomfort might God be calling you go? What would your response look like if God was calling you to go there?

2. What are the primary obstacles impeding your willingness to respond to God's Misfit Mission for your life?

3. If you could strip away all of your current obligations or fetters (job, mortgage payment, retirement, etc.), what God-sized dreams would you be willing to claim for your life?

1. Bobbi Jo Reed, *Beautifully Broken* (CreateSpace Independent Publishing, 2014).

CHAPTER TWO

JUST SAY "YES!"

The caller ID function on telephones came into existence in 1989. However, most of us had to wait until 1993 before we could add this "high tech" function to our phones. Given the opportunity, most of us added it. Who wouldn't want to know who was calling them before they picked up the phone?

Fast forward three decades and here we are living in a world of smartphones, complete with apps like Skype, Face-Time, Snapchat, and others that make it nearly impossible not to know who is calling. Knowing who is calling is normative. In fact, it's actually gotten to the point in my life where I instinctively check to see who is calling before the thought of answering the phone crosses my mind, and I typically won't answer the phone if I don't know who is calling. My wife is the same way. We knew we were in trouble when we discovered that our very first home's landline didn't come with caller ID. Can you believe that? Who doesn't have caller ID on their phone?

Those were precious times in our marriage. Whenever the phone rang, no matter how hard we tried to guess, we never knew who was calling or why they were calling, for that matter. Every time the phone rang, we found ourselves wondering anxiously, "Who is calling us? It's 8:30 at night! What could possibly be wrong? Who could they want now?"

After a while, it got to the point that the phone would just ring and ring and we would just sit still and wait, paralyzed by our fearful wonderings. Inevitably, I always answered because Wendy would convince me that it was somehow "my turn." It was always my turn. This became a nightly routine for us and, I hate to say it, but it didn't stop with the phone either. We went through the same routine anytime someone unexpectedly rang the doorbell or knocked at the door.

I don't know if eventually installing caller ID on all of our devices solved our marital issues, but it has made us a little more comfortable with the unknown numbers or knocks of this world, but even still we have a hard time answering calls when we don't know who's calling. Then again, sometimes knowing who's on the other end of the line doesn't always make it easier to answer. There are actually times when knowing who's calling makes it more difficult to answer. Have you ever experienced that?

The phone rings, you look down to see who's calling, and it's a name you recognize. Maybe it's a friend who's upset with you. Maybe it's your boss. Maybe it's a loved one bearing bad news. Whoever it may be, upon seeing their name, you suddenly discover that you're not ready to answer. The next thing that happens is the conversation in your head that begins saying something like, "Oh, I'll talk to them later" or "I can't talk with them now." What do you do? You probably do the same thing I do: press the "ignore" button, sending that person (your friend, co-worker, spouse, or acquaintance) straight to voicemail.

I don't know whether it's hesitation, avoidance, or downright procrastination, but we sometimes have a hard time answering calls even when we know who's calling.

What do you do if it's God calling you?

God Is Always Calling

The God of the universe *longs* for us. God consistently and frequently urges and invites us to do the very same things that God does. God calls us and equips us with the ability to bear lasting fruit regardless of who we are, where we are, or what kind of phone we can afford.

Have you heard the phone ringing?

Have you answered any of God's calls?

The truth is this: God is always calling.

One of the first things I had to believe upon helping to get Resurrection Downtown started was that I was worthy to be called. Being able to say and actually believe that I was worthy of God's call was imperative.

Do you believe this? Do you believe that you are worthy of God's call?

You should.

You are worthy of God's call and invitation.

17

The most foundational dimension of God's Misfit Mission is **believing that you are worthy of God's call and invitation.**

Prior to my time at Resurrection Downtown, my life was such that I didn't always believe this. I didn't always believe that I was worthy of God's call—or anyone else's for that matter. I didn't want to answer the phone. I was reluctant, hesitant, and fearful, not because I didn't know who was calling me, but rather because I didn't believe I was worthy of the invitation. I didn't reach five feet in height or one hundred pounds in weight until my senior year in high school. I was smaller than most, which made me feel less than most. I thought, "Why would God, or anyone else for that matter, ever call a person like me?" This caused problems in my early life with friends, classmates, family, and even my faith. It didn't matter who you were, I generally sent everyone to voicemail, God included, because I didn't feel worthy of the invitation. I didn't want to take the call.

This is the beauty of God's Misfit Mission. God doesn't call the equipped, but rather God equips the called, namely the wrong people, which means that we are all worthy of God's call and invitation. God invites us all, regardless of who we are, to join in God's Misfit Mission.

When I decided to leave my career in finance and investments in order to pursue a life of ordained ministry, something changed in my life and I actually began responding to God's invitations no matter how surprising they were. It got to the point whereupon moving to Kansas City, I embraced a new policy for my life regarding this foundational dimension of the Misfit Mission. I called it my "Just Say Yes" policy.

"Just Say Yes" Policy

In the first days and weeks on the ground in Kansas City, I would start each day repeating to myself, "I am worthy of God's invitation." I said this over and over again (under my breath). The result of this repetitive mumbling was that it shaped the way I saw everything. I began living a life that viewed everything as opportunities to answer and accept the invitations that came my way. I simply said, "Yes!"

Whenever I received an invitation or was asked to join someone or some group of people on some sort of adventure, I would say, "Yes."

Do you want to go grab a cup of coffee? *Yes.*

Do you want to go for a walk? *Yes.*

Do you want to see a Snoop Dog concert? *Yes!*

The "Just Say Yes" policy led me to experience all sorts of things I never would have imagined. I experienced professional bull riding and loud hip-hop concerts. I heard the ear-pounding sounds of a NASCAR race. I peered into Major League Baseball dugouts and sat mere feet from big league ballplayers. I've spent time in jail, in homeless camps, and in multimillion dollar estates, experiencing life with the down-trodden as well as the upper crust of Kansas City.

One of the craziest invitations I accepted within the first few months of meeting people in Kansas City was taking part in a four-day hiking trip to Colorado with a small group of guys. Our purpose was to go backpacking through Rocky Mountain National Park. Our goal was to tackle our first ever "Fourteener," which is an ascent to the top of a fourteen-thousand-foot mountain peak.

"Do you want to join us?" they asked me.

Instinctively, I whispered under my breath, "I am worthy of God's invitation," as I mulled their invitation. After a few moments, I assumed this had to be God calling, so I responded saying, "Yes! I'm in."

After a few months of preparation (climbing stairs in heavy boots while holding weights), we trekked to the base of the mountain. Our plan was to split the hike into two days. We spent the first day hiking half of the way. We set up camp at 12,500 feet in a boulder field and were hoping to summit the mountain on the morning of the second day. How hard could it be?

I remember getting to the campsite after the nine-mile hike on the first day. I was short of breath and shivering. I underestimated the elevation gain and the impact of a sixty-pound backpack. As I looked around the campsite, longing for a cozy place to pitch my tent, I noticed a sign that offered everyone planning on camping a warning. It read something along the lines of "Hike at your own risk because it is possible that you might die on this mountain!"

Mercifully, the next day we all woke up very much alive and eventually we clambered to the top. But once we made it to the top, we still had to hike back down. I didn't anticipate or expect that the descent actually would be much scarier than the hike up. Going down the mountain, I could actually see where I was going to die should I lose my footing!

After numerous slips, falls, and near misses, we made it. But during the entire descent I kept on repeating, "Guys, this is crazy! I have no business being on this mountain. What are we doing here?" I wasn't fit for something like this. I'm not a fan of heights and I was not properly prepared for this kind of adventure. So, I echoed time and time again, "Guys, this is crazy! I have no business being on this mountain."

The frequency of my statement, of course, increased the more tired I became. Over and over again, I said, "Guys, this is crazy!" Eventually I had said it enough that the strangest thing happened. It might have been the fatigue or my simple inability to clear repetitive songs from my head, but while coming back down the mountain my frequent complaint morphed into a refrain from a popular song (amongst teenage girls) by Carly Rae Jepsen. So there I was, tired as can be and trekking down a fourteen-thousand-foot mountain with a sixty-pound pack on my back for nine excruciating miles, and all I could think, hear, or sing was, *"Hey, I just met you. This is crazy! Here's my number. Call me maybe."*

If you haven't heard it, the song is a pop classic, a totally emasculating one at that.

"And all the other boys try to chase me. But here's my number. Call me maybe."

For four hours I continued to sing this song under my breath, though I was just loud enough to annoy each one of my hiking mates. I'm not condoning this song (as I lost a lot of credibility with my friends for singing it ad nauseam), but one thing I learned about this song as I sang it repetitively while descending my fourteener is that it actually describes God's Misfit Mission.

In order to live fully and experience God's life-giving power and presence we must believe we are worthy of God's call, as crazy as it seems, and we must also be willing to say, "Yes!"

I learned this upon reflecting over an accomplishment I never thought to ask for or imagine: successfully summiting a fourteen-thousand-foot mountain without injury. But this fourteen-thousand-foot journey was nothing compared to the crazy call stories in scripture.

Contained within both the Old and New Testaments are numerous stories where God calls fatally flawed people to join in God's transformative mission. Consider that none of these flawed people are what we (or any expert) would ever envision or imagine when we think about changing the world or achieving God's purposes, and yet each one of them grew to believe they were worthy of God's call, even as misfits, and because they did, the craziest things began to happen. Let's start with Moses.

Moses

Moses is one of the most revered biblical figures in the entire Bible. But Moses was also a child born into unfortunate circumstances. Shortly after being born, he was abandoned by his mother, placed in a papyrus basket, and floated down the Jordan River in the hopes that someone might rescue him from both the river and the hopeless life he would have had as a slave under Egyptian control. Sure enough, someone did—Egyptian royalty, in fact. The pharaoh's daughter picked him up, took him in, and raised him as part of their royal family. And yet Moses, even though his life was privileged and pampered, was always troubled by the mistreatment of the Hebrew people (his people), slaves under Egyptian control. One day he witnessed a slave being beaten by an Egyptian, and Moses lost control of his emotions, rushing to the defense of the abused slave. In his enraged defense, Moses killed the Egyptian (cf. Exod 2:11-12). Moses became a murderer. Fearing the consequences of his actions, Moses fled from Egypt to the land of Midian hoping to find refuge and shelter. But that is when things got really crazy!

A bush burst into flame and a voice called, "Moses! Moses!" Not only did a bush burning with an "inconsumable fire" speak to Moses, but it called his name—twice (Exod 3:2-4). In order to get our attention, God always calls us. God's call is the one that doesn't stop after the first ring. It keeps on ringing until we, eventually, *have* to pick up. "Moses! Moses!" And Moses can't help but answer the phone saying, "What do you want?!"

Out of the burning bush, God shares what he wants to do with Moses:

> I've clearly seen my people oppressed in Egypt. I've heard their cry of injustice because of their slave masters. I know about their pain. I've come down to rescue them. (Exod 3:7-8)

The natural assumption for anyone reading this story, or in Moses's case, standing before this fiery bush, would be that God would continue this call by describing or announcing in great detail how God would go ahead and do this in God's unfathomable and unlimited power and might. But that's not what happens at all. Instead, God, who created the universe, who can literally do all things, and who has just set this bush afire in perpetual blaze, says to Moses, "And in order to do set my people free, I am sending you," or more specifically *"I'm sending you"* (Exod 3:10).

23

I imagine Moses's reply to be something like, "Excuse me? What was that again? You're s-s-s-sending whom? It's odd be-be-be-cause I thought you said M-M-Moses."

God replies, "That's exactly what I said, Moses. I am sending you to confront the all-powerful Pharaoh, the person from whom you are fleeing, the person who wants to persecute you, the person who will definitely bring punishment and retribution upon you for murdering that guy in Egypt. I am calling you to deliver my people from Egypt!"

It's at this point in the story when Moses started to sing quietly and nervously under his breath, *"Hey, I just met you, and this is crazy..."*

This is God's way. It is crazy!

The God of the universe chooses us, as crazy as it seems, as terrifying as it seems, to do these extraordinary things! Moses was fleeing from his shame and guilt. He had killed a man out of (righteous) anger and now he was an exile. Moses was of no use to any of the Hebrew slaves. The only people who seemed to appreciate him weren't even people—they were sheep. Moses was a misfit, and yet God was calling him.

"Moses! Moses!"

God's Misfit Mission begins when we believe that we are worthy of God's call, and then respond by saying, "Yes!"

At first, Moses didn't believe he was worthy. In fact, Moses asked God, "Who am I that I should go to Pharaoh and bring the Israelites out of Egypt?"

God replied by saying, *"You are mine. Moses, you did not choose me, but I have chosen you and appointed you. You shall not go empty-handed. I will be with you (I will equip you, train you and be with you)... the whole time."*

Despite his doubt, uncertainty, and fear, Moses found the courage to respond. He said, "Yes."

By the grace of God and because Moses believed himself to be worthy, he became the one who delivered the Israelites from slavery at the hands of the Egypt in order that they might journey into Canaan, the land of milk and honey. Moses's life ended on the top of a mountain, but before he perished, he stood on the summit of Mount Nebo looking out over God's promised land, and he praised God for the crazy and unimaginable adventure where he was able to accomplish far more than anything he could have ever thought to ask or imagine (cf. Deuteronomy 34).

Moses was one of God's biggest misfits who believed he was worthy to be called and had the boldness to simply say, "Yes!" So was Jeremiah.

Jeremiah

In Jeremiah 1, God calls Jeremiah, who is just a boy. Upon hearing God's call, Jeremiah answers. God quickly and clearly establishes God's own identity and the plans and purposes for Jeremiah's life. God said,

> Before I created you in the womb I knew you;
> before you were born I set you apart;
> I made you a prophet to the nations. (Jer 1:5)

That's when the line went quiet. Jeremiah hesitated, wondering, "What do I say? How should I reply? Does God have the right guy?"

As the silence lengthened, I imagine that Carly Rae Jepsen's song began creeping into Jeremiah's mind. *"Hey, I just met you, and this is crazy."*

25

What God was saying was absolutely crazy. So, Jeremiah broke the silence by protesting and questioning God's invitation, saying, "Ah, LORD God, I don't know how to speak because I'm only a child" (Jer 1:6).

However, God wasn't deterred by Jeremiah's age and insecurity and continued the call by jarring Jeremiah's memory, reminding him who God is and who he is. God then tells him, "Don't say, 'I'm only a child.' Where I send you, you must go; what I tell you, you must say. Don't be afraid of them, because I'm with you to rescue you" (Jer 1:7-8).

Like Moses, Jeremiah ultimately responded to God's call by saying "Yes," and because he did, Jeremiah experienced God's life-giving power and presence. This teenage misfit in all of his inexperience became known as one of the most prolific prophets throughout the Old Testament. He became known as the one who indeed plucked up and pulled down, destroyed and overthrew, built and planted (Jer 1:10). Jeremiah became the prophet who reminded Israel and all of us of God's plans. God spoke through Jeremiah to all of us saying, "I know the plans I have in mind for you, declares the LORD; they are plans for peace, not disaster, to give you a future filled with hope" (Jer 29:11).

In the end, Jeremiah believed he was worthy of God's call, and he responded by saying, "Yes!"

This same kind of storyline occurs all throughout scripture in both the Old and New Testaments. One sees similar things happen to Jonah. Rather than responding with reluctance, Jonah simply took off running in the other direction. It wasn't until he found himself languishing in the belly of a whale that he found the courage to believe that he was worthy to be called, and he responded (cf. Jonah 2). Upon doing so, Jonah, by God's grace, saved an entire city.

Similar things happened to Hosea, Hannah, David, Jacob, Rahab, and Paul. None of these figures had great wisdom, training in diplomacy, or royal heritage. All of these people were normal and ordinary. They were people like you and me. I might suggest they were insignificant or unsuspecting people, by all means the wrong kinds of people by the world's standard. They were misfits, and yet God chose them in order to accomplish extraordinary things.

If Moses was inept, if Jeremiah was afraid, if Jonah was unlikely, then there must have been an obvious flaw in Mary as well!

Mary

Mary was a single, unwed woman in a culture and context that ascribed very little worth to her status. She was one of the least in terms of society's pecking order. In fact, out of all the scriptural heroes, she was probably least likely to be called. This is what happened to her according to Luke:

> When Elizabeth was six months pregnant, God sent the angel Gabriel to Nazareth, a city in Galilee, to a virgin who was engaged to a man named Joseph. ...When the angel came to her, he said, "Rejoice, favored one! The Lord is with you!" She was confused by these words and wondered what kind of greeting this might be. The angel said, "Don't be afraid, Mary. God is honoring you. Look! You will conceive and give birth to a son, and you will name him Jesus. He will be great and he will be called the Son of the Most High. The Lord God will give him the throne of David his father. He will rule over Jacob's house forever, and there will be no end to his kingdom." Then Mary said to the angel, "How will this happen?" (Luke 1:26-34)

27

God approached this young, unsuspecting woman and told her that she was going to bear the Son of the Almighty God. Mary replied saying, "How can this be? *I just met you, and this is crazy!*"

God reassured her, "Nothing is impossible with God."

Then the Spirit of the Lord came upon her. Mary believed herself to be worthy and responded boldly, saying, "I am the Lord's servant. Let it be with me just as you have said" (Luke 1:38). From that point forward she began to live a life that sang aloud a song much more magnificent than Carly Rae Jepsen's classic. Her whole life began to sing a song that magnified the Lord.

Mary is a genuine example of faith acted out in attentiveness and response to God's call. If Mary's ears had been any less keen and her soul any less willing, the world might not have understood God's power and presence. If her eyes had been able to see only the self-deprecating outlines of her own insecurity, if she simply focused on the upcoming trial, tragedy, rejection, and hardship she would have to face, we might not have ever sensed the divine presence or heard God's word of grace and favor in our own lives. Mary's story reminds all of us misfits that the craziest invitations are packed with God's promise of greater things. In the same way that God's solitary call fuels this mission, our response, our willingness to answer the call, becomes the spark that sets off amazing transformation and life change.

What would have happened if Mary didn't answer? What would have happened if Mary believed that she wasn't worthy of God's invitation?

When we know God's voice and answer God's crazy call in light of who we are, we are able to sing, and as our soul "magnifies the Lord," we ourselves are magnified, becoming greater than the sum of all our parts (Luke 1:46). We have the ability to share the light of Christ or the image of God to the world around us.

What is God calling you to do? Can you hear God? Have you answered? Believe you are worthy and say emphatically, "Yes! Here I am, Lord. Send me" (cf. Isa 6:8).

Discussion Questions

1. With the three previous call stories in mind (Moses, Jeremiah, Mary), do you believe you are worthy of God's call?

2. What is causing you to doubt or second-guess that you are, in fact, worthy of God's invitation to change the world?

3. If you could respond one of God's surprising invitations, worthiness or unworthiness aside, what would it be?

ALL ARE INVITED: NOT JUST THE LEAST AND THE LOST

There is no such thing as the science or art of successful leadership in the Bible. When you look for patterns, recipes, or the seven habits of highly effective leaders, you won't find them in scripture because there is not a science or formula for scriptural leadership. Instead, what scripture teaches us about fulfillment, purpose, calling, faithful discipleship, or leadership is that in order to find it or live into it, you most necessarily have to be a misfit. This is God's Misfit Mission.

Bishop Will Willimon, a leader within The United Methodist Church, suggests that "the people who are called to lead, who live most fully, who are the most successful in Scripture are almost always the wrong people."[1] In a previous chapter, we remembered how God generally chooses the ill-equipped "nobodies" of the world, people who most would consider unworthy to be called. We remembered Moses, Jeremiah, Mary, and the Misfit King himself, Jesus.

If we unpack the stories of other patriarchs, we'll discover that Jacob was deceitful, Paul persecuted Christians, and David was the absolute runt of the litter. Fast forward to the Gospels and we'll discover that even the first disciples were the wrong ones. They were "nobodies." They were fishermen among other things. God has a preference for the unlikely choice or "the wrong people," as Willimon suggests.

It goes against the merit-based nature of our American culture to conceive of leadership, discipleship, or success in this way, but this is how it works. God's Misfit Mission begins not with our own ambition to accomplish, lead, or succeed, but with God and, specifically, God's personal invitation. As Jesus says in the Gospel of John, "You didn't choose me, but I chose you and appointed you so that you could go and produce fruit and so that your fruit could last" (15:16). Therefore, in order to lead effectively we need to understand that God is actually the one leading the way, and God goes before us with God's sacrificial life and love.

God leads us on the Misfit Mission by loving us and never leaving us. God's love is unconditional, unwavering, and, most importantly, sacrificial. God is a leader who always places the self-interest of others above all else. This is love and this is what it looks like to lead effectively: to lay down your life for another. In order to become a misfit engaged in God's mission to transform the world, we must sacrifice our own self-interests and ambition in order to focus on and follow God. We must let go of who we are and instead focus first on who God is, what God does, and then strive to reflect God's image to the world around us by doing the same things.

This is easy if you don't have any ambition, social standing, or power. This becomes easy if you are already considered a misfit or a "nobody" by the world's standard, but what if you are a "somebody"? What if you have power, influence, social status, and a lot to lose? Though God certainly seems to have a preference for the poor, lowly, downtrodden, and outcast, God also calls and invites the somebodies of this world.

Most of the people who experienced God's call didn't come from a position of perceived power; they were by the world's standards the "wrong people." But God also calls the "right people," and responding to God's Misfit Mission can be difficult as a person of power or prestige. In Luke 9:23-27, Jesus shares with his disciples a picture of this difficult pathway forward by saying,

> All who want to come after me must say no to themselves, take up their cross daily, and follow me. All who want to save their lives will lose them. But all who lose their lives because of me will save them. What advantage do people have if they gain the whole world for themselves yet perish or lose their lives? Whoever is ashamed of me and my words, the Human One will be ashamed of that person when he comes in his glory and in the glory of the Father and of the holy angels. I assure you that some standing here won't die before they see God's kingdom.

Does this galvanize you into action?

Or does this cause you to shy away?

God's Misfit Mission is challenging to those who are considered to be people of power and authority. Consider Pontius Pilate, the rich young ruler, the chief priests, scribes, and Pharisees. These are people with position and with established power and wealth. Seeing Jesus Christ for who he was (God in the flesh) or even for who he claimed to be (more powerful than anything they could ask or imagine) would have stripped them of everything they had. Confessing Christ as Lord or living lives that proclaimed "God is God and I am not" would have forced them to lose it all. So, more often than not, they didn't. Pontius Pilate washed his hands of it (Matt 27:24). The chief Priests and scribes cried out, "Crucify him" (Matt 27:20-22). The Pharisees rejected Jesus and the rich young ruler ran away (Matt 19:16-22).

God's Misfit Mission is embodied by the ethos, "No one has greater love than to give up one's life for one's friends" (John 15:13). This kind of life galvanized some into action, but it alienated others. The truth is that God's call actually applies to everybody near and far, big and small, rich and poor, sick and healthy. We are all misfits. We are all God's, as opposed to gods. Regardless of who you are (sick or healthy, rich or poor, powerful or powerless), God is calling you to be a part of this Misfit Mission. God created *you*. God loves *you*. God is calling you, and there is absolutely nothing *you* can do about it—except respond.

In order to live into God's Misfit Mission, we need to do the very hard work of actually acknowledging that God is God and that we are not. We need to be aware of God's presence and power. Like Moses, we need to see the burning bush (cf. Exod 3:2), or like Isaiah, we need to see the Lord on the throne, and then answer by confessing, "I'm here; send me" (Isa 6:8). When this happens, even the most successful, powerful, authoritative figures (the likely candidates for leadership by the world's standards) can become God's most notable and surprising misfits called into the mission of changing the world! One example of this can be found in Isaiah.

Isaiah 6: I'm Ruined!

In the sixth chapter of Isaiah we get our first sense of what it looks like for someone of power to become one of God's misfits. As the chapter begins, Isaiah, the mighty prophet of God, enters into the Hebrew temple, a place and institution where he had power and authority. As he entered into a place that could be considered to be his home, something out of the ordinary happened. Isaiah saw something. He was confronted by something much bigger than him.

Isaiah writes with clarity,

> I saw the Lord sitting on a high and exalted throne, the edges of his robe filling the temple. Winged creatures were stationed around him. Each had six wings: with two they veiled their faces, with two their feet, and with two they flew about. They shouted to each other, saying:
>
> "Holy, holy, holy is the LORD of heavenly forces!
> All the earth is filled with God's glory!"
>
> The doorframe shook at the sound of their shouting, and the house was filled with smoke. (Isa 6:1-4)

It was a powerful scene, all of which forced Isaiah to his knees. He cried out before God and everyone watching, "Mourn for me; I'm ruined! I'm a man with unclean lips, and I live among a people with unclean lips. Yet I've seen the king, the LORD of heavenly forces!" (Isa 6:5).

Isaiah, a man of power and authority, had given it all away by acknowledging that God is God and he was not. God is greater than anything we could possibly imagine. God is more prominent and powerful than we could ever be. Isaiah described God's presence as being so big that only the hem of God's robe fit inside the temple, and the angel voices could be heard so clearly and so powerfully that their simple song caused the foundations of the temple to tremble. The combined power of all of this forced Isaiah to physically fall down. It was too much for him to handle. So he had to confess. He had to worship! He finally became a misfit.

What was once strong, authoritative, and powerful had become weak. What once was first had become last. A "somebody" (by the world's standards) had become a "nobody." On his knees, Isaiah bowed down in humble admonition in order to offer a powerful confession, "Mourn for me; I'm ruined! I'm a man with unclean lips." Isaiah finally acknowledged that he was one of God's chosen misfits.

Isaiah took a posture of humility and ultimately confessed that God was leading the way forward. It was from this point in his life that Isaiah went on to lead the children of Israel, sharing prophetic visions of holy anticipation of One who was greater than he.

Becoming a part of God's Misfit Mission requires that, regardless of our perceived power, position, or authority, we understand ourselves to be misfits (God's, not gods). It means realizing that any power we might hold isn't ours, but God's. Any physical or intellectual abilities or financial capabilities we have aren't actually ours—they are God's. Our careers, social status, success, or perception of power are all rooted not in our own efforts or merit, but in the almighty power of the God who created all things seen and unseen, whose robe is so big that its hem alone can fill up the holiest of temples.

Reorienting our lives in this way, acknowledging that God is God and that we are not, and seeking to glorify God by loving and serving God through all that we are and all that we've been given forces us to not only see ourselves as God's Misfits, but allows us to reflect God's image to the world around us. This in turn makes possible a future where the eyes of the blind are opened, where all those with ears might hear, and all those shackled in the valleys of shadows, darkness, and death might find light and life.

You can see this happen in Isaiah's life, and what I love about Isaiah in particular was that he began as a person of power. He was then humbled by God's presence and power. I think that is what makes Isaiah so extraordinary. He risked everything he had in order to respond to God's call, and he had a lot. This only magnified his life-changing impact.

Isaiah, a person of power, responded to God's call, but there were others as well.

In the Gospel of Luke, up until the twenty-third chapter, Jesus's life had been poured out amongst the nobodies, the outcast, and marginalized (people with nothing to lose). Jesus dined with sinners, broke social protocol with tax collectors, and was defiled before the law by touching the unclean. He cared for the marginalized and they followed him, worshipping him and glorifying God through him, but the story shifts in Luke 23. Our attention turns from the marginalized and oppressed and turns toward people with power, position, or wealth, just like Isaiah.

The Centurion

The Roman centurion is the first figure Luke focuses on after Jesus's death. Centurions were perhaps the most organized and powerful military force of that day and age, using new tactics and formations like the phalanx to subjugate most of the known world. Centurions were officers and by no stretch of the imagination, ultimate fighters. After Jesus breathes his last, the centurion is the first figure we meet. The truth is, however, we met him earlier as he stood before Jesus as he died, casting lots to divide up Jesus's clothes (Luke 23:34). We heard his voice as he mocked Jesus saying, "He saved others. Let him save himself if he really is the Christ sent from God, the chosen one" (23:35).

But later in the twenty-third chapter, the centurion is markedly different. Luke writes,

> Certainly this man was innocent. (Luke 23:47 NRSV)

By the power of the Holy Spirit or through the mystery of Jesus's death, this centurion, a social giant, having seen and experienced Jesus's death, has changed. At the cross, the centurion praised God and proclaimed Christ's innocence, thereby admitting his own guilt. Like Isaiah centuries earlier, the centurion fell to his knees and confessed his faith in God in front of the other Roman soldiers, all of his direct reports, and the angry crowd. In the presence of God and all these people, this strong and mighty centurion becomes a misfit, conscripted into God's Misfit Mission by stating, "Certainly this man was innocent!"

This was a stunning moment of public conversion. This was transformation in the flesh. This was the holiest of holy surprises. This was worship. In the Ancient Greek, worship was understood by the word *proskuneō*, meaning "to bow down" or "to bend the knees." Worship in ancient Greece was nothing more than an act of humbling oneself, confessing, or repenting. Worship was sacrificing who you are in order that you might acknowledge God for who God really is. It's admitting that God is God, and we are not. This is what the Roman centurion did in the sobering aftermath of Christ's death. He humbled himself. He bowed down. He worshipped publicly and became a misfit called to God's mission.

In death, the centurion, like Christ, found new life. He didn't lose his position, he did not change his line of work, but from that moment forward this centurion began living his life differently. Though he was still a centurion, he no longer lived for himself (or for Tiberias Caesar) but for Christ.

News of the centurion's conversion spread like wildfire in ways that impacted the world then and continue to impact the world now, more than two thousand years later. That a person of prominence like a Roman centurion would humble himself and live a life that sought to bear the image of God was extraordinary. Things like that didn't happen. It was surprising, if not revolutionary. This is the power of God's Misfit Mission.

The centurion wasn't alone in his unexpected conversion. There were other social giants out there who had similar experiences in the days that followed Jesus's passion on the cross.

The Crowd

After the centurion left, there was still a crowd of people standing near the cross. Luke continues, "All the crowds who had come together to see this event returned to their homes beating their chests after seeing what had happened" (23:48).

This group was similar to the centurion. It was made up of socially important people: the rich young ruler, the young attorney, chief priests, and scribes. These religious, economic, and political powerbrokers of Jesus's day had also witnessed the crucifixion. They, too, were immersed in the darkness of Christ's death. In fact, they had put him there. And, yet by the power of the Holy Spirit, while standing or milling about Golgotha, these people also experienced the newness of life. Luke records that this crowd left confessing, repenting (beating their breasts), or, in other words, worshipping. In the shadow of the cross and in light of God's sacrificial love, the powerful crowd became God's newly minted misfits called into mission just like the centurion. The result was momentous as news of their conversion spread quickly throughout the land.

However, they weren't alone either. In addition to the Roman centurion and the powerful crowd, there was also a man named Joseph, from Arimathea.

Joseph of Arimathea

Joseph was a good and righteous man according to the Hebrew law. He was a member of the council and was involved in all of Jesus's pretrial festivities. Joseph of Arimathea was an important person in the religious landscape of Jesus's day. He was wealthy and responsible. Joseph was also a part of the voting body that put Christ on trial, but he didn't agree with the actions of the council (23:51). After witnessing Jesus's horrible death, Joseph stood alone in the darkness, wringing his hands. It was here that Joseph would do an extraordinary thing. Joseph of Arimathea had a reaction similar to that of the centurion, but even more profound.

> This man went to Pilate and asked for Jesus' body. Taking it down, he wrapped it in a linen cloth and laid it in a tomb

40

carved out of the rock, in which no one had ever been buried. (23:52-53)

In the grim aftermath of the crucifixion, Joseph responded in an unexpected and humble way. First, he visited Pontius Pilate, the Roman authority who had sentenced Jesus to death, and asked for Jesus's body. He wanted to place Jesus's innocent body in Joseph's very own family tomb.

This act itself was significant because by simply trying to recover Jesus's body (the property of Rome) Joseph was risking his social status. Many people don't realize this about Joseph. His request of Pontius Pilate alone would have been enough to threaten his hard-won place in sight of Caesar. By asking for Jesus's body, Joseph would have been honoring a convict, a rebel, someone whose ministry threatened the stability of the society that gave Joseph his power and standing in the first place. However, Joseph was also compromising his well-earned standing under the law of Moses. By asking for the deceased, Joseph was declaring that he was willing to handle the dead, which would have rendered him unclean, powerless, and ultimately uninvited from the Passover feast. This was unheard of amongst Jewish officials, let alone any of the faithful. This kind of response would have severely undermined his social standing amongst his fellow Jews in light of God's law.

The Gospel continues as Joseph followed through with it. He made good on his inquiry and risked everything he had and all that he was in order to bury Jesus honorably and mercifully. Joseph of Arimathea became a misfit.

While Joseph was immersed in the darkness of Jesus's death, he experienced the life of Christ and began to live differently. From this point forward, Joseph sought to go and do likewise: to lay down his life for his friends. Joseph of Arimathea sacrificed everything he had: his status, his standing, his wealth, and his power in the sight of both Rome and Israel in order to participate in God's Misfit Mission by placing Jesus Christ in the burial tomb. Joseph was God's Misfit in Mission. He was willing to do the very thing that so many people were afraid to do.

And that's the lesson we learn from each of these successful or powerful individuals. The centurion, the powerful crowd, and Joseph all risked their lives to follow Christ, in order to pave the way for a larger story or a future filled with hope and resurrection life. They used the gifts God had given them, their position and power, in order that God would be glorified and that the whole world might experience the promise of eternal life. This is what it looks like to be a Misfit in Mission, to be God's, not gods.

Once Jesus's earthly ministry came to an end, after having spent all that time with the people society deemed to be the "wrong" people (the downtrodden and oppressed, the marginalized and sick), the people who appear to be "somebodies" join the ranks as well. They sacrifice everything they have in order to find the life that really is life. They, too, become misfits.

The Roman centurion, the powerful crowd, and Joseph from Arimathea, were the first people of power associated with God's Misfit Mission, and in the process they become the first people to celebrate Easter.

Have you experienced this kind of transformation?

When I moved to Kansas City, I was overwhelmed. I found myself in the darkness of a new town, without friends and family, without a church community, and without much of a picture of a pathway forward. I had lost all of my status, social capital, and familiarity—the things that made me feel like a somebody—and yet I believed that God was calling me. That didn't mean things were easy. In fact, I wondered if I should go back to Michigan.

My friends and family were there. I had familiar power like the centurion, like Joseph of Arimathea, like the Pharisaic crowd. People knew me, supported me, missed me, and loved me there. Or I could stay in Kansas City, trusting that God reserves the best work for moments like these where the darkness of doubt and death surrounds us. I had a choice to make: I could resolve to live a life that proclaimed "God is God and I am not" and seek simply to serve those around me by doing the things that God did, or I could go back home.

In the end, I eventually resolved to trust in God's promise of eternal life and love over and against my own perceptions of power, status, and familiarity. I wanted to be God's, not a god. I knew it would require a lot of hard work. It would require everything I had and all that I am, but this is the life that Christ calls us to, one of sacrifice, unconditional love, and a resolve to do whatever it takes for the glory of God.

Discussion Questions

1. God calls "somebodies" and "nobodies" into God's Misfit Mission; with whom do you most identify? Why?

2. Do you believe that you are God's Misfit? Is it easy for you or difficult to imagine that God is calling you to change the world?

3. Does your life reveal that God is God and you are not? If so, how? If not, what might you do in order to better reflect God's image to the world around you?

1. William H. Willimon, "Back to the Burning Bush: Leadership 101," *Christian Century*, April 24, 2002.

CHAPTER FOUR

SO YOU'VE SAID
"YES!" . . . NOW WHAT?

T
he Secret Life of Walter Mitty, starring Ben Stiller and Kristen Wiig, arrived in theaters on Christmas of 2013; it was a remake that tells the story of a guy named Walter Mitty. Walter spent his whole career as a negative assets manager for *Life* magazine. Walter was someone who had worked for the same company in the same role for his entire career. His life was predictable, controlled, and neat. His imagination, on the other hand, was not.

Walter Mitty, like so many of us, had a secret life filled with hopes and dreams of doing great things and going to great places. In his mind, he imagined himself to be someone living an adventurous life. In reality, though, Walter never actually did anything.

Jesus says, "I assure you that whoever believes in me will do the works that I do. They will do even greater works than these" (John 14:12), and the Apostle Paul assures us by saying that by the grace given to us we are able to accomplish unimaginable things. Living into these promises constitutes God's Misfit Mission. God created and shaped us that we might reflect God's image to the world around us, and God calls us into this work by inviting us to do the same things that God does.

What are you doing? Are you breaking free from your everyday nine-to-five or are you stuck doing the same thing over and over again?

I used to watch SportsCenter nonstop around the clock. Every hour on the hour, I tuned in to hear the same sports reports over and over again. This was my escape. Over time, I found that I began to pay more attention to the commercials than to the program itself. Some of my favorite commercials were ones that depicted mascots from several major collegiate and professional athletic teams functioning in their regular day-to-day routines. These commercials featured mascots at "work," immersed in a regular nine-to-five, oftentimes frustrated at their circumstances and their inability to break free to be the people they were.

One commercial in particular always caught my attention. It was subtle, but it helped to open my eyes to the life I had been leading before the ministry. In it, the Oregon Duck (from the University of Oregon) was sitting at a desk in the middle of a sea of cubicles positioned next to a window overlooking a pond filled with actual ducks. As the Oregon Duck typed away at his desk, he heard the ducks quacking in the pond outside his window. There they were, making noise and having fun in their natural environment. Upon hearing these ducks, the Oregon Duck realized he was stuck at work and he would never be able to sit on the pond with those other ducks. He sighed in defeat. He was stuck at work, and his life was passing him by.

Have you ever felt like this duck? Do you ever look out the window and want to be with the other ducks?

In *Ferris Bueller's Day Off,* Ferris (the main character, played by Matthew Broderick) is a senior in high school who takes the day off from school. His life motto was, "Life moves pretty fast. If you don't stop and look around once in a while, you could miss it." Ferris was not like the Oregon Duck. He did everything and anything he wanted. He took the day off from school, drove around in his friend's dad's Ferrari, caught a foul ball at a Cubs' game, and ate lunch with friends at an expensive restaurant.

Ferris Bueller is Walter Mitty's opposite. Ferris never missed an opportunity to enjoy life or to live fully.

Have you ever wished you could live like Ferris? Have you ever wanted to break free from the monotony in order to experience holy adventure?

Sometimes our life, or our life's work, causes us to forgo dreams, shackle our lives, or restrict our potential. Sometimes it even paralyzes us.

Nigel Marsh, business leader, speaker, and author of several books on the matters of work and life, shares,

> There are thousands and thousands of people out there leading lives of quiet, screaming desperation, where they work long, hard hours at jobs they hate to enable them to buy things they don't need to impress people they don't like.[1]

A June 2013 Gallup poll suggested that more than half of American workers who have full-time or part-time employment (52 percent) are less than satisfied with their work.[2] Are you like more than half of American workers?

The truth is that a great majority of working men and women are stuck living lives of quiet, screaming desperation, which is exactly how the man sitting outside the pool of Bethsaida felt in John 5.

The man beside the pool of Bethsaida might not have been shackled by his work, but he was certainly stuck. Everything passed him by: people, opportunities, and life. There he was at the Sheep's Gate in Jerusalem. Beside it was the pool of Bethsaida, thought to have cleansing and healing powers. His life and his future was sitting right there, but he couldn't get there.

> A crowd of people who were sick, blind, lame, and paralyzed sat [under the five covered porches]. A certain man was there who had been sick for thirty-eight years. When Jesus saw him lying there, knowing that he had already been there a long time, he asked him, "Do you want to get well?" The sick man answered him, "Sir, I don't have anyone who can put me in the water when it is stirred up. When I'm trying to get to it, someone else has gotten in ahead of me." Jesus said to him, "Get up! Pick up your mat and walk." Immediately the man was well, and he picked up his mat and walked. (John 5:3-9)

The first thing to notice about this story is that this verse does not specify the man's illness. The root of this man's suffering or "stuckness" is not known. The only thing we could possibly know is that the man has been stuck or has at least felt stuck in the same place for thirty-eight years.

Can you imagine that?

38 Years . . .

Many biblical scholars look at this number and think about this man's "stuckness" as an indication of permanence.

This man's affliction and suffering felt permanent. He was permanently hopeless.

What must it be like to feel permanently hopeless or without hope for thirty-eight years?

Thirty-eight years is longer than I have been alive. Thirty-eight years ago, Elvis Presley was still the king of rock. Jimmy Carter was still president. The United States was just entering into the Cold War, and the Challenger space shuttle had not yet exploded.

Can you remember that far back?

It seems like forever.

This man had been stuck forever, and then along came Jesus. Longing to heal this man, Jesus walked right up to him and asked directly, "Do you want to get well?" Jesus had no prior knowledge of this man. He didn't know his name or affliction. He didn't care how long he'd been there. All Jesus wanted to know was whether this man desired to be made well.

Rather than offering a simple "yes," the man became defensive. He replied, "Every time I try to get up to do great things or to go great places, other people cut in front of me. I don't have anybody to help me! Nobody here loves me!" Instead of answering Jesus's simple question, this man bemoaned his predicament.

Upon hearing him, Jesus paused. He looked at him once more and replied with three very direct instructions. He said, *"Get up! Pick up your mat and walk."*

Through these words, Jesus called, equipped, and encouraged him to become the person he was created to be: a person called and equipped to do the things that God does, to reflect God's image everywhere he goes. "Get up! Pick up your mat and walk," Jesus said, setting him free to live forward as one of God's Misfits in Mission.

Immediately, the man does as Jesus commanded, and for the first time in thirty-eight years, he begins living fully into the future without fear, the future that God has for him, a future filled with hope. He goes places he's never been before and does things he's never done. He walks forward with the confidence of God's call to go and do likewise, equipped to reflect God's image to the world around him.

This is one of the more dramatic healings in the Gospels, but in all honesty, the drama comes not on account of the man's physical healing. This story becomes dramatic because of its timing. Although the man has been stuck for thirty-eight years, Jesus decided to heal this man on the Sabbath.

News of this Sabbath healing began to spread throughout the land and as it did, the Jews resolved to kill Jesus. Jesus had broken Torah and defiled God's holy Sabbath. The Jews wanted retribution for Jesus's blatant disregard for the law. They wanted to punish Jesus for calling, equipping, and encouraging this man into life. From this point forward in the Gospel of John, Jesus was forced to flee from the considerable reach of the religious leaders of his day for fear of what they might do to him.

Why Couldn't Jesus Wait a Day?

Things took such a violent turn after Jesus healed this man by the Sheep Gate that it forces us to wonder why Jesus didn't wait a day to heal this man. At this point in Jesus's ministry, there was still a lot more he could have done without the threat of death chasing him everywhere he traveled. Certainly he could have waited one more day, right? After all, this man had been stuck in the same place for thirty-eight years! What was one more day? What would that have hurt? Jesus could have leaned over and whispered to the man something like, "Meet me here tomorrow morning, and I'll help you then. I promise."

Why didn't Jesus wait?

It Is Always the Right Time

With Jesus, *it is always* the right time to start doing the things that God does. It is always the right time to start living in response to God. It's never the wrong time to wake up to God's redemptive power and enter into God's Misfit Mission. The time is always right to believe that you are worthy of the call and start living in a way that reflects God's image to the world around you. There is no reason to wait, and yet most of us wait.

The overwhelming reality for untold millions of people is that we hit the workforce around the age of twenty-two (or immediately upon graduating from college, trade school, or something else). And from the moment we begin working, we start dreaming of the day when we will have earned, saved, and accumulated enough to finally start living in retirement. If you start working at the age of twenty-two and retire at a target age of sixty, then this means you'd be waiting at work for thirty-eight years before you can begin to really live.

Is this your reality?

Nigel Marsh posits that there are millions of people out there who feel stuck like this in the status quo. The good news is that Jesus challenges this. God's Misfit Mission flies in the face of this. Jesus confronts us and calls us, just like he does with the man on the mat, with urgency saying, "Get up! Pick up your mat and walk."

Whether you've been at the same job or running the same race for thirty-eight years, thirty-eight months, or thirty-eight days, Jesus longs to meet you and give you the grace needed to live fully. *The time is always right to start doing the things that God does.* Don't wait a day longer. Don't sit idly by, but instead hear the call, believe you are worthy, and respond to it by getting up, picking up your mat, and walking. Take risks. Go for it. Live forward faithfully into the future God has for you and experience God's misfit and holy adventure of bearing God's image wherever you go because this is where you will experience abundant life. This is where you'll experience the life that Jesus refers to when he describes himself as this very same gate. In John 10:9-10, Jesus tells the crowds that

> I am the gate. Whoever enters through me will be saved. They will come in and go out and find pasture. The thief enters only to steal, kill, and destroy. I came so that they could have life—indeed, so that they could live life to the fullest.

In the same way Jesus met the man at the pool of Bethsaida, he longs to meet you. Jesus longs to meet us at work, not so that we might all quit our jobs, but so that we might view our work differently, namely as the primary place where we can reflect God's image to the world around us.

Leaving one's career is not required in order to become a part of God's Misfit Mission. A life of discipleship, God's Misfit Mission, and our ability to reflect God's image to the world around us does not and should not hinge upon our jobs or occupations. We do not need to leave our jobs or careers in order to become the best versions of the people God longs for us to be. The truth is that God longs for us to find value and meaning in the work we do. Our work helps us to live into the fullness of who God created us to be. It is the pathway toward life if only we could see it as such. Work can be good, if we view it differently.

In a 2012 study, Dan Ariely described how researchers have discovered something they called "the IKEA effect."[3]

IKEA makes and designs furniture that requires a lot of time and patience to assemble, but once people have finished putting together their IKEA furniture, they almost always like it better than the other pieces of furniture in their house, namely the pieces they didn't have to assemble themselves. Why does this happen? Because they had to work in order to assemble their IKEA furniture, which points to a simple truth that says, we find increased value and meaning in the work we do.

These same researchers found that a similar thing happened with cake mixes in the 1940s and 50s. The first-generation cake mixes came to the market in the late 1940s. These mixes contained all the ingredients needed to make a cake (eggs, milk, butter, and so on). The only thing required for the earliest cake mixes was that you must add

53

water (or milk). How simple was that? Much to everyone's surprise, these first cake mixes were largely unsuccessful. They didn't sell well at all. So, the cake mix companies pulled them off the shelves and went back to the drawing board. A few months later, they changed things up a bit. In addition to taking away eggs and some other ingredients, they added instructions to the side of the box, telling people what they needed to do in order to bake a cake. These second-generation cake mixes required people to do more work, and they began flying off the shelves. Why? Because we find value, meaning, and life in the work we do.

One can see this elsewhere, too, with surgeons, engineers, entrepreneurs, and artists. The things they (and we) build and the work they (and we) do has an increased value depending on the time and effort required for completion.

Perhaps the best example of the increased value we place upon work would be the work we do to build and grow our families. Think about kids and the kind of value they have in this life. Could you even put a value on them? For parents, it's our children who carry the utmost value. They are our life's work.

This is also how God values us. Regardless of our jobs or occupations, we are God's priceless work. God finds meaning and joy and life in us and, moreover, God created and called us to do the same things God does and to feel the same way God does about God's work as well.

In the beginning of time, when life was perfect and God spoke all things into being, God formed and shaped us. On the sixth day God created humankind in God's image (Gen 1:26-27). At our most basic level we are bearers of God's image. Like large mirrors, we were created with a capacity

54

to reflect the image of God and God's light and life to the world around us. This is the work that God calls us to, and the good news is that this work transcends our job titles. We can do this kind of work everywhere. This is our real work. We are called to bear God's image by doing the things that Jesus did: loving others the way God first loved us. This is God's Misfit Mission.

Jesus's mission was to love us and never leave us. Some people say Jesus came to die, but this is simply not true. Jesus came first to love, but sometimes the excruciating byproduct of Jesus's love is death, and yet even in death people can experience the depth of his love. Nothing can separate us from the perfect love of God, not even death (cf. Rom 8:38-39).

On the cross, in death, Jesus's heart was broken and poured out so that the entire world could experience this love. This was Jesus's life work: to love us and never leave us, to go with us even to the end of the age (Matt 28:20). In John 17:4, Jesus cried out to God,

> I have glorified you on earth by finishing the work that you gave me to do.

Jesus's life's work was to glorify God by revealing God's perfect love for the whole world to see, so that we might experience worth, love, and life. Work was not just another four-letter word for Jesus, but it led him toward one. Jesus's work, his perfect love, leads us all to the life that really is life. As God's Misfits, we ought to see our work as a pathway that leads toward the same thing.

Our life's work is to do the things that God does: to love one another the way that Jesus first loved us. This is God's Misfit Mission and the good news is that we—not just the prequalified—are all called to this type of work. God calls all of us to serve one another and love one another the same way that Christ loved and served us, and it has nothing to do with our jobs or occupations. We can do this kind of work no matter our employer. We can do God's work as a volunteer, in retirement, wearing blue collars, white collars, clerical collars or any other kind of collar, as Jesus reminds us:

> You are the light of the world. . . . Let your light shine before people, so they can see the good things you do and praise your Father who is in heaven. (Matt 5:14-16)

We are more than our jobs and occupations.

One of my favorite television shows is called *Dirty Jobs* on Bravo. The whole point of the show is to follow along as the show's host, Mike Rowe, temporarily works at what most would consider horrible jobs and occupations. We follow along as he goes on the jobsite with roadkill collectors, catfish noodlers, and septic tank technicians, among others.

One would think that both he and the people he works alongside would be miserable because of their work, but they're not. I've watched and enjoyed this show since it first began airing and what you will find is that these people are generally happy and full of life. They enjoy what they do, not because of the gritty tasks or general messiness, but because of how they can see it meeting the greater needs of the world around them. They can see how they are contributing to the bigger picture of the world around them. They can see how they are changing and improving the world. In most cases, these dirty job employees are living sacrificially, serving and working in a way that makes it possible for others to fully live and in that way they have become much more than their jobs. They are living reflections of God's image to the world around them.

Mike Rowe discovered something in the midst of life's dirtiest jobs: joy, peace, and life. He discovered that if he did something that made people's lives better, even if it was boring, routine, or insignificant, he was living in a way that led toward the life that really is life. I would contend that he was fulfilling God's Misfit Mission. The work we do isn't about titles or trajectory. It is about seeing whatever we do as a means toward reflecting the image of God to the world around us by doing the same things God does. When we do these things, when we view our work in this way, when this becomes our daily mission, we will find life.

When I look out at the community at Resurrection Downtown on Sunday morning as they gather for worship, I see a collection of septic tank technicians, CEOs, attorneys, students, builders, and artists. I see a collection of God's Misfits; they don't belong together, except that they do. The individuals at Resurrection Downtown don't view themselves or each other as being defined by their work. Instead they view themselves as a group of individuals who were created, called, and equipped by God to do the things that God does: to bear and reflect God's image to the world around them by living and loving sacrificially so that others might see their good works and give glory to God.

Let me be clear: **in order to live into God's Misfit Mission, you do not need to leave your job.** You do not need to switch professions because the truth is that you are more than your job. Before you were a doctor, lawyer, pastor, retiree, student, or banker, you were created. You are God's craftsmanship. God has created you in God's own image. You are God's good creation, called and equipped with the mission to simply do the things that God does. So be fruitful. By your love for those gathered around you, bear fruit that will last and lead people to life (John 15:16).

One of the things most people wrestle with is the question of *what should I be doing with my life?* However, that isn't the question misfits ask. The question God's Misfits ask is not *"What should I be doing with my life?"* but rather *"How am I glorifying God, through my work? How is what I am doing reflecting God's image to the world around me?"*

Paul invites his church at Ephesus to remember why they are working and how they should be acting on the job. He says,

> Don't work to make yourself look good and try to flatter people, but act like slaves of Christ carrying out God's will from the heart. (Eph 6:6)

Paul says to his church at Colossae,

> Whatever you do, do it from the heart for the Lord and not for people. (Col 3:23)

"Whatever you do, do it from the heart for the Lord," writes Paul. Work first for the One who calls you to bear God's image always and everywhere. Whether you are employed, retired, or still in school, God calls you to do the things that God does wherever you are; this is your work. The job itself is secondary. Our identity as God's craftsmanship, or God's misfit creation, is always primary.

Paul demonstrated this approach to work everywhere he went. The whole time he was building churches throughout the Mediterranean, his occupation was a tent-builder (Acts 18:3). Building tents was his "job." However, Paul knew that he was more than his job. He was one of God's Misfits called and equipped for God's transformative mission. He knew his purpose or the pathway toward life.

When Paul was asked, "What do you do?" he didn't reply, "I make the best tents on this side of the Jordan River." He talked about the perfect love of God or Christ crucified. Then again, Jesus would have been the same way. Jesus also had a "real job." Whenever people asked him about his profession, did he reply talking about his carpenter skills, or did he talk about his Father in heaven?

How do the people in your community know you? Perhaps you should ask ten people.

Do they know you as an engineer or accountant or do they know you as God's servant?

I was sitting at a local children's hospital in their Center for Genomic Research. I was there to visit a parishioner. I normally visited patients at this children's hospital, but that day was different. I was there to visit the director of the Center. As I sat there, I began to realize that I was in way over my head in terms of having a firm understanding of what actually goes on in a place like that. You can imagine my anxiousness. The whole time I sat and waited, I was praying to God that I would make it through all of my upcoming conversations about genomics, DNA research, and the politics of it all. However, no such conversation ever took place.

This highly successful director of genomic research wanted nothing to do with conversations about genomic research. Instead he wanted to know about how he could glorify God through his work.

He asked me, "How could I most effectively glorify God through my job here as a director of genomic research? How can I be fruitful in terms of reflecting God's image to my colleagues? How should I approach my work? How should I talk to my co-workers and clients? How should I lead them? How much time should I spend at work, at home, with my children, in my community, at my church? How should I measure success?" His questions left me speechless. These are the kinds of questions God's Misfits should ask. They shouldn't worry about what they do, but rather how they are glorifying God through whatever it is they find themselves doing.

Those who consider themselves as God's craftsmanship won't worry about what they do, so much as how they glorify God through it. Becoming one of God's Misfits requires that we remember our primary work will always be Christ's, in the same way that Jesus understood his life to be rooted not in his work as a carpenter, but in his ability to live into his Father's work.

Regardless of what you do, your job or occupation, Jesus tells his disciples and all of his Misfits to remember

> You are the light of the world. . . . Let your light shine before people, so they can see the good things you do and praise your Father who is in heaven. (Matt 5:14-16)

The greatest work that we can do, generally speaking, has nothing to do with our jobs, our titles, or our careers, but how frequently we engage in the hard work of remembering that we are God's. We are God's Misfits, people whom God has called and equipped to bear God's image to the world around us—always and everywhere, no matter what. So "Get up! Pick up your mat and walk." Don't wait another day. God is calling, equipping, and encouraging you to live fully into the opportunities and occasions surrounding you wherever it is you go and whatever it is you do. Simply do the things that God does always and everywhere and start now!

What does that look like for you?

How are you reflecting God's image?

Naturally, this looks different for every one of us, largely because God gifts us and equips us in misfit ways that are totally unique for each of us as individuals.

Janelle is a young mother from Kansas City with a full-time job. She is successful, competent, and filled with a capacity for changing the world, and yet she felt something was missing. An inner voice told her there was more that she could be doing. She wasn't living a quiet life of desperation, but she felt she could do more. She prayed and looked for opportunities to get outside the walls of her nine-to-five, to do the things that God does out in the world around her, to glorify God in all that she does and all that she is. Then something crazy came before her. Someone asked her if she would be willing to shine shoes at a local bank in her spare time because of her great personality and ability to be hospitable.

Janelle was actively employed but was looking to get outside. And she thought, "What better way to step out than by serving those around me, kneeling, serving and shining shoes?" After all, Jesus also had a propensity for washing feet. For the past ten years, the act of shining shoes on Fridays has become for her a means for finding life and changing the world. Through the conversations she has and the relationships she creates, Janelle is changing lives and finding hers to be changing in the same way. However, it took stepping up, stepping out, and saying yes to the opportunity at hand in order to find abundant life through a different kind of work. Shining shoes isn't work for Janelle. It is not just another four-letter word. It is an avenue where she can now do the things that God does in an unconventional way, outside the walls of her nine-to-five. She can love and serve others in ways that makes friends out of strangers and in turn builds community and bears fruit in powerful ways.

This second job and holy adventure has inspired her to do all sorts of adventurous things. She's now traveled internationally in mission. She's met hundreds, if not thousands, of people she never would have met before, and she's grown to understand her life differently now that she spends time serving people by shining their shoes. She believes her life to be better because of it.

However, the answer for everyone isn't to shine the shoes of the people around you.

Sarah is a mother of two and also works part-time. Sarah has a degree in journalism and is extremely high capacity, in that she excels in almost everything she sets her mind to. As Sarah spent her life working part-time, parenting two children, and being a loving spouse and a good employee, she, like Janelle, felt something was still missing. She felt stuck at home. She felt like she was shackled by doing life's most important work of all, raising children. Rather than simply resigning to this work, she decided to do something more.

Sarah looked for ways to use her gifts that would take her beyond the routine of being a part-time employee and full-time mom. Being a journalism major, Sarah started to write. She began blogging to the world around her about her experience as a mother who longed for more. What she quickly realized was that there were a whole bunch of other moms out there who felt the same way but were afraid to say it. Sarah's words quickly began to spread and her experience continued to resonate with the world around her, and all of the sudden she realized that she was serving others and loving others, reflecting God's image and shining God's light in ways she could have never imagined. Her blog took off and she found fulfillment.[4] Sarah has since invited other mothers to join her and to do the same thing so that no mom in Kansas City feels alone, but rather surrounded and encouraged to do similar things, to do the things that God does and accomplish abundantly far more than anything they could ask or imagine by taking risks, being bold, and living faithfully into the future without fear.

When I think about people who have been set free into living the life that really is life, I think about the leaders of church programs and outreach initiatives to public schools— all of whom do this outside of their regular nine-to-five jobs. I think about a group of people at my church who spend time on Friday mornings stuffing worship bulletins or the hundreds of volunteers who staff our children's ministries. I think about people who, when asked, would mention these activities as the things that bring them the most amount of life and energy.

Every time I recall the story of the man laying beside the pool at Bethsaida, I think about Jesus's command. But more than that, I envision the man running free and without fetter from his comfortable cubicle or portico and how it must have felt for him. I picture him running with reckless abandon, a smile on his face, living fully in light of God's call to pursue the life that really is life.

God's urgent call to each and every one of God's Misfits is, "Get up! Pick up your mat, and dive into the world around you! Do not wait one more day." Join the other ducks, spend time with your family, love others the same way that God first loved you, and live into the world around you at work, at home, and with your friends and families in a way that glorifies God by the work you do. It doesn't matter what you do—just that you are doing something. Paul reminds us,

> Whatever you do, do it from the heart for the Lord and not for people. (Col 3:23)

Blog about your life. Shine shoes, switch careers, switch cities, or simply serve in the church. Just get going, whatever it is that you do, and reflect God's image to the world around you.

Discussion Questions

1. How are you glorifying God through your daily job or profession?

2. What can you be doing in order to push past the boundaries of your nine-to-five in order to live fully?

1. Nigel Marsh, "How to Make Work-Life Balance Work," *TEDxSydney*, May 2010, www.ted.com/talks/nigel_marsh_how _to_make_work_life_balance_work.

2. Gallup.com, June 2013.

3. Dan Ariely, "What Makes Us Feel Good About Work?" *TEDxRiodelaPlata*, October 2012, www.ted.com/talks/dan _ariely_what_makes_us_feel_good_about_our_work.

4. Sarah McGinnity, http://kansascity.citymomsblog.com /author/kcmomsblog/.

CHAPTER FIVE

STARTING OUT SMALL: PUTTING TOGETHER YOUR OWN MISFIT MISSION

Not too long ago I was invited to speak at a conference working with several church leaders in Honduras. Before this trip, I had never delivered a message or told a story with the aid of an interpreter. Preparing for this event, I imagined a scene much like a United Nations, where everyone wore headphones as interpreters from a variety of nations spoke as quickly and as quietly as they could into the ears of their respective delegates listening in. I imagined a scene where there was no break in the action at all.

Once I arrived in Honduras, I was rushed to the first gathering without any time to prepare. As I walked into the conference center, without any time to even take a breath, it was my turn to speak. So, I picked up the microphone, stood to address the crowd and started to share the story of Resurrection Downtown. Surprisingly, I felt on top of my game. I was telling stories without stuttering and feeling fairly confident. But after a few minutes of speaking, I noticed something rather alarming. The crowd wasn't offering any favorable feedback. Instead they appeared to be struggling a bit. They looked quite frustrated and confused. Upon noticing their confusion, I also noticed that none of them were wearing hearing assistance devices and that there didn't appear to be any interpreters present whatsoever. So, I turned and looked around. Eventually my eyes connected with another other person standing up a little ways away from me on the stage. When our eyes met, he shrugged his shoulders and said, "Pastor Scott, I'm sorry. I'm your translator and I didn't get any of that. You're going to have to slow down your speaking and pause every couple of sentences so that I can translate for the crowd."

I was confused, terrified, and what's worse is that I had forgotten what I just said. I made the mistake of saying that out loud as I confessed to my translator, "*Oh no! I don't remember what I said!*" This, of course, prompted his first and perfect translation to the crowd, which caused them break out in laughter. So, there I was with all of these stories to tell and all of it had been lost in translation.

Have you ever felt as though you had so much to offer but no way to live into it? Like you have a message to share but all you end up with is one big mess? This is the beginning of your own Misfit Mission.

Resurrection Downtown is a community that began just like this. We had these great big visions and dreams, but in reality we were a simple collection of just nine individuals. We were small and disorganized. Our present reality hardly compared with our God-sized hopes and dreams and yet, in five years time, what began as just a handful of individuals has grown into a community that worships with one thousand adults weekly. Of those one thousand people, about half are under the age of thirty-five, about 40 percent are above the age of forty-five, and the remaining 10 percent are somewhere in between. We are multiracial, socioeconomically diverse, have lots of kids, and are growing every day by the grace of God. But it didn't start out like that.

When we started we didn't have much of anything. We didn't have any people and we certainly didn't have a space to call our own. It was this way for the first eighteen months. Resurrection Downtown was totally mobile and virtually invisible until we purchased our first building: a former bar/concert venue. A few years after that, we opened up a second site, with a second sanctuary, offices, and several classrooms. Our second site was a former Canon copier company building.

When I think of our community and the path it took to get to where it is, I am continually humbled (and quite possibly baffled) because Resurrection Downtown started out the same way my speech in Honduras did—without much power. We had vision but no people. We had ideas and stories to share but no translator. We felt called but not qualified, and yet this was God's way.

What We See Matters

Henri Nouwen writes,

> A Christian leader is not a leader because he announced a new idea and tries to convince others of its worth; he is a leader because he faces the world with eyes full of expectation, with the expertise to take away the veil that cover its hidden potential.[1]

Our vision, what we see, rests at the heart of the Christian faith, and this matters most in the beginning of any adventure or in those moments when our present circumstance or realities are small. Our vision is central. Not only did Resurrection Downtown have an extremely small beginning, but so did I. I didn't hit one hundred pounds in weight until I turned eighteen years old. The same thing held true for my ability to surpass the five-foot mark in height. My life and my ability to move forward required that I believe I was more than what I saw in the mirror. I needed to imagine my life as filled with God's unlimited possibilities that would most definitely surpass my present and very small start.

The stories in scripture remind us that God lifts up the least and the lost. That God spends time breathing life into the imperceptibly small and insignificant. God called forth Jacob, the second born, to carry forward the promises of God over and above his older brother Esau (cf. Genesis 25–33). God blessed a misfit like Joseph, the twelfth brother who was sold into slavery and left for dead by his other brothers, in order that he might carry God's people forward through famine and drought (cf. Genesis 37–50). God chose Jeremiah who was just a boy and Mary who was just a girl. I had to believe that God did the same for me.

The kingdom of heaven works in a similar fashion. In Luke, Jesus described the kingdom of heaven like a mustard seed. He said,

> [God's kingdom is] like a mustard seed that someone took and planted in a garden. It grew and developed into a tree and the birds in the sky nested in its branches. . . . [God's kingdom is] like yeast, which a woman took and hid in a bushel of wheat flour until the yeast had worked its way through the whole. (Luke 13:19-21)

The kingdom of heaven is something that starts out extremely small, perhaps as small and insignificant as we are, only to later grow into something extravagant. Even Jesus's ministry took place in a very small geographic region. Most of his miracles, healings, and sermons happened within three cities that take up a combined area of approximately 6.5 square miles. Jesus's mission and ministry started out small and yet it grew to the point that it continues to impact us two thousand years later. God's call shares the same dynamic in our life. When the phone rings in our lives, God's call usually starts out small, even though most of the time we are expecting something huge.

Small Beginnings

God calls and equips us into mission that has the power and potential to change the world, but oftentimes the Misfit Mission begins as imperceptibly and subtly as God's own people do. In order to see it, one must be on the lookout for it. We must live in search of God's possibilities; however, searching is very different than actually seeing. Seeing God's possibilities can be something of a struggle. It has been since the beginning of Jesus's ministry.

Throughout Jesus's life most people couldn't or wouldn't recognize Jesus for who he really was. When people encountered Jesus, rarely did they see the Son of God. Instead they saw a rule-breaker. They saw someone unclean, out of his mind, obsessed with the poor, evasive, controversial, and even threatening. Rarely, if ever, did people actually imagine that he might actually be the Messiah or the Lord.

71

Jesus described the people surrounding him throughout his ministry as having eyes to see but being unseeing (Mark 8:18). They could look but never perceive or understand. People's first impressions rarely matched the realities they were facing. People couldn't see God's possibilities even when they were standing in front of them in the flesh.

Jesus experienced this deficiency everywhere he went. One place in particular happened in the sixth chapter of John. Jesus had just fed five thousand hungry souls with five loaves of bread and two fish. After that, Jesus managed to walk on water in the middle of a violent storm. Upon returning to shore, Jesus was immediately confronted by the same hungry crowd from the day before. They asked him for more food saying, "We're still hungry. We've run out of bread to eat, Jesus. Can you do what you did before?"

Instead of obliging their request, Jesus asked them a simple question, not about food, but about their vision. Jesus asked them, "Do you see who I am?"

In the Gospel of Mark, Jesus said to them,

> Why are you talking about the fact that you don't have any bread? Don't you grasp what has happened? Don't you understand? Are your hearts so resistant to what God is doing? Don't you have eyes? Why can't you see? (Mark 8:17-18)

Jesus wanted to know what they saw. Were they seeing the Messiah or did they simply see McDonald's? Did they see the Son of God or did they simply see Mary and Joseph's son?

Jesus didn't let them answer, but instead reminded them that he is who they were looking for. He says, "I am the bread of life" (John 6:35). In other words, Jesus is the one who will offer them more than they could ever possibly need. And then he points them directly onto the pathway toward life, saying,

> This is the will of the one who sent me, that I won't lose anything he has given me, but I will raise it up at the last day. (John 6:39)

Seeing and Believing

"All who see the Son and believe in him will have eternal life" (John 6:40). In saying this, Jesus made it clear what they need to do in order to experience the life that really is life. They simply needed to see the possibilities of God standing before them. They needed to see and believe in what was standing before them, they needed to see and believe in God's possibilities right then and there. However, rather than taking a deeper look or taking the time to really get to know the Son of God, they began to question Jesus all the more saying, "Isn't this Joseph's son? Who is he that he now claims to come down from heaven?" They had eyes, but they couldn't see. We are the same way.

We all have eyes, but we don't always see, perceive, or understand the power and possibilities of the present realities we are facing, and there are consequences attached to this. By not seeing the power and possibilities of God, we miss out. Our lives remain the same: empty, hungry, unfulfilled. I like to think that given an opportunity like the disciples I would be successful in recognizing Jesus for who he was, but I'm not so sure I would. Rarely do we push past our first impressions or preconceived notions in order to uncover God's power or potential. Rarely do we take the time to push past the surface in order to dive deeply into God's possibilities all around us.

In Matthew 25, Jesus reminds his disciples and us that every time they do something for the least of these, they do it for Jesus. Every time they visit someone in prison, befriend the least and the lost, feed the hungry and give the thirsty something to drink, they do it for Jesus (Matt 25:31-46). When Jesus told his disciples this, they questioned him just like the Jews did in John 6. Even the disciples weren't aware of Jesus's presence always and everywhere. They were serving, loving, befriending, and sacrificing for the least of these, and even as they engaged in those acts, they missed out. They too had eyes, but could not see. Jesus reminds them, and us, that he was there, is there, and forever will be present in the world around us. Our task as God's Misfits is to simply see and believe.

The Apostle Paul says that we are to live life by fixing our eyes not on

> the things that can be seen but on the things that can't be seen. The things that can be seen don't last, but the things that can't be seen are eternal. (2 Cor 4:18)

Our ability to focus on unseen things and to move according to the convictions of these things is imperative in our pursuit of God's Misfit Mission. This is what it means to walk by faith and not by sight. We are called to focus on the unseen things, trusting that God's power and possibilities (eternal things) are resting beneath the surface wherever we go.

At our first official gathering as RezDowntown (an informational gathering), Wendy and I posed with nine other individuals for a picture. This was history, and I remember thinking how unimpressive this gathering would be to outside observers. (Church experts suggest that successful church starts require a launch team of at least fifty people.) Standing pat at nine people, we were shy of that "suggested milestone" by forty-one people. However, as I continued looking at those nine people I began thinking that this group might be small in number, but I believed that we were large in spirit. You couldn't see it upon first glance, but as I gazed at this picture, I thought that here were nine individuals who committed to starting a church without a critical mass. They were bold, courageous, and strong. They were ready and excited to do something crazy. They didn't fit any mode or model, and what's more, and they didn't care. As I gazed at this gathering of misfits ill-equipped for the mission at hand, I realized that their presence alone revealed the size of their heart. So I paused and prayed at our gathering and every gathering that followed, inviting people to join me in prayer saying,

> *God remind us to always focus not at what can be seen but at what cannot be seen; for what can be seen is temporary, but what cannot be seen is eternal. Lord, help us to remember that you see possibilities even when others cannot. That surrounding us throughout this city are people who long to see you and be transformed by you. Use us to build community and to change lives in this mission field by the grace of Jesus Christ.*

This simple prayer still guides us to this day, and it continues to inform most of the decisions we make at Resurrection Downtown because in order to live fully as one of God's Misfits in Mission, we must possess a willingness to look past the predictable in order to focus on things unseen, God's unlimited possibilities.

E. Stanley Jones, a prolific Methodist preacher, often talked about the life of discipleship in visual terms as well. As he traveled in mission, speaking to people all over the world about the grace of Jesus Christ, Jones often spoke of the importance of knowing the difference between gazing and glancing. He said that as we go through life we look, scan, or glance from side to side, and we see things that capture our attention from time to time. That's normal. However, our glances should always give way to our gaze. Our prolonged gaze should always be fixed upon God's power and possibilities (or the grace of Jesus Christ).

God's Misfits in Mission should glance at problems, but we should gaze at solutions. We should glance at obstacles, but gaze at our goals and finish lines. It's okay for God's Misfits to glance at all sorts of things like cars, money, politicians, sports, or wealth, but in all things, no matter what the circumstance, we should fix our gaze on God, not on what can be seen, but what cannot.

God's Misfit Mission is rooted in our vision, our focus: in what we can see, and where we fix our gaze. In all things we are to remain focused on Christ, constantly fixing our gaze upon God's possibilities. And then we are to invite others do the same.

Our Vision Shapes Every Decision

It is difficult to fix our gaze on the power of God always and everywhere. Sometimes it is easier to focus on obstacles.

It is instinctive for us to focus on fear, grief, all that we don't have, or all that prevents us from finding joy, fulfillment, and satisfaction. These are things that we are prone to glance at from time to time. However, problems will arise when these glances turn into gazes.

Have you ever experienced this?

What are you focusing on currently?

Are you seeing problems, obstacles, or impediments?

Or are you focusing on God's possibilities?

Focusing my eyes and actions on things unseen shapes the person I am now. What I see informs every decision I make, but especially when it comes to hiring people to join my staff team. This was one of the first things I focused on after meeting the small group of nine. I needed to find some help. I needed to get some people onto our staff team quickly. But who?

I was looking for a director of operations and had received a stack of polished résumés, people with all of the right qualifications. When I met Kelly, she had none. She didn't have formal experience and she didn't have any relevant training or education, but she had a giant heart and eyes that could see and believe. Kelly was the kind of person who was willing to do whatever it took to meet people where they were in ways that made everyone feel comfortable. Kelly could even see that in me. Very early on, Kelly actually saw that I was floundering without anyone there to support me, keep me organized, and focused outwardly. She saw something in me that most others couldn't—namely that I needed help, that I was a misfit too. This turned into an opportunity for Kelly. She didn't see an impediment; she saw God's possibilities. She believed God was calling her, in spite of her qualifications, to serve at Resurrection Downtown because of what she saw and believed.

Kelly didn't have a résumé, but she had ability to see things that others could not and she was determined to do whatever others would not in the hopes that life would abound. Kelly is the type of person who has always focused on the possibilities within all the people dancing around her no matter where she is or whom she is with. She is hospitable, loving, and funny. In her prior life, she was a full-time Christian comedian. During her stand-up routines, she could spend twenty minutes improvising on the most mundane details of life that nobody ever noticed and draw endless laughter from unsuspecting crowds. This is who Kelly was. No polish or practice, no past experience, but she knew the difference between gazing and glancing. She both saw and believed in God's possibilities.

Kelly joined our staff team as our director of operations working just ten hours a week. Her job description was simply to do whatever it took to meet people wherever they were in ways that would invite them to experience God's possibilities even in the smallest of ways. Kelly was my first misfit, somebody most people wouldn't have hired, and yet she was ripe with God's possibilities. She is now our longest tenured staff person and largely responsible for a lot of Rez-Downtown's success. Had I simply stuck to looking only at the practical or predictable résumé instead of pushing past our first impressions onto the things unseen, I hate to imagine where RezDowntown might be today.

Upon first glance, a polished résumé or storied experience always tempts and entices; however, the "right" hire is never found in the first glance. Focusing only on what we can see (résumés and experience) will always leave you wanting more, but when we take the time to push past first impressions in order to go deeper, we begin to uncover unseen things, eternal things, or God's unlimited possibilities.

After Kelly was hired, I began to systematize our criteria for determining the "right" candidates for our staff team. I put together a list of hoped-for attributes for all new staff. These are the unseen things we constantly search for even today.

The Five Things We Look For

We look for **commitment.** We search for the type of people who are "all in" and 100 percent committed to God's mission of creating Christian community where non-religious and nominally religious people can become deeply committed Christians. We see our ministry as the most important work we could be doing and are willing to do whatever it takes to fulfill our commitments to the ministry. Being fully committed means offering all that you have and all that you are for the sake of God's call to change the world.

In addition to being committed, Resurrection Downtown is determined to find people who understand and demonstrate a commitment to **holistic living.** We search for self-aware individuals who understand what they individually need in order to be the best versions of the people they were created to be. We look for people who can articulate their individual needs (improved spiritual discipline, physical exercise, diet, social relationships, retreat, and so on) and are willing to work collectively to hold one another accountable to fulfilling our individual commitments of meeting those needs. These kinds of people would hold a primary posture toward others of support, encouragement, and love.

Additionally, we search for people who are **invitational**. A great danger for a church, a staff team, or any disciple for that matter is to become insular and exclusive. Resurrection Downtown is determined to uncover the type of people who aren't. We are looking for individuals who practice radical hospitality and will be invitational in every aspect of their lives. We want people who will model ways for our community to be inclusive of others and invitational everywhere they go in order that others might come and see God's possibilities.

We look for **authentic humility**. We long for people who lead authentically and humbly. We want people who do not consider themselves to be better than anyone else. We want people who don't pretend to have all of the answers. We look for people who will always maintain a posture of learning and will strive to always think the best of others. In fact, one of the first questions I ask potential candidates after they've met with the team is, "What have you learned so far?" The second question I ask is, "What will I learn about you after you've been on our staff for six months?" I love the answers I hear to these two questions, as they reveal a lot about one's humility!

80

Lastly we long for people who understand the importance of **playfulness**. We avoid taking ourselves more seriously than we should, and we look for others who will do the same. We search for people who can find creative ways to incorporate playfulness into their daily work. In our office we have a four-square court, we host movie days, and we bring in treat bags for our staff to enjoy. Each week we nominate all-day all-stars. We put up pictures of hip-hop and R&B recording artist Usher Raymond in our "Usher Closet." Anything goes in terms of keeping things light and playful, and one of our favorite mantras is that nothing is too serious that a game of four-square can't interrupt. We long for people who can be playful and take joy in fulfilling their call to change the world by the grace of Jesus Christ.

Our second staff person embodied each one of these attributes, even though he wouldn't have been considered as a possible candidate upon first glance.

I was looking for a part-time worship leader and I was hoping for somebody great! I wanted a polished and experienced worship leader who had the potential to change the world with world-class stage presence, and then I met a guy named Neil, on Craigslist of all places.

Neil was an amazing musician (jazz saxophone), who was living locally while working toward his PhD in saxophone performance with a cognate in jazz studies. He was twenty-six years old, newly married, and looking for a job (at least that's what he said on Craigslist). I quickly discovered that Neil was actually looking for something more. As newlyweds, Neil and his wife were looking to meet new people, make friends, build community, and ultimately form bands that could play gigs around town. Neil had a heart for connecting with other musicians and he was looking for ways to do this for a living. This was exactly what we needed our first worship leader to do. I needed someone who saw every person he met as an opportunity. Neil lived life this way. He saw every stranger as a potential friend and every musician as a potential member of his worship team. His life was defined by his call to make friends out of strangers using his gift and passion for music as a backdrop.

Like Kelly, Neil could see things that others couldn't. He formed and shaped bands of students and musicians in order to lead worship together, regardless of their experience within the church. By his résumé alone, Neil was somebody that most people would have passed over, and yet he was ripe with a vision that allowed him to see and believe. He saw God's possibilities in others wherever he went.

The same thing has been true of almost all our staff members. They have come far and wide, not with great résumés or experience, but with hearts fit for doing whatever it takes and eyes that are able to see God's possibilities even when others cannot.

This is true of our congregation as well. Just like Jesus, they love to be interrupted by small, imperceptible, almost unseen people and things, in order to uncover God's unlimited possibilities. This is their call: to fix their gaze upon the things unseen, just like Jesus. Everywhere Jesus went, he stopped and healed, stopped and resurrected, stopped and taught, or stopped and prayed. Jesus was always open to holy interruption because in them he could see abounding possibility. This is our congregation.

One example of this involved a fourth-year medical student who had been a part of our church for only a few months. One Sunday night she attended worship dressed in her workout clothes. I remembered seeing her walk into service late (like in the middle of my sermon), but didn't think much of it until I saw her standing and waiting in line to talk with me after worship. Once she got to me, I asked what brought her here tonight. She shared with me that she was out on her evening run through the city (she had planned on skipping church in lieu of running), and she came across a distraught woman. This woman caught her attention and forced her into a place where she had to make a decision: "Do I keep running?" or "Do I stop and see what's going on?" Instead of running past her, she stopped. She asked her if she needed any help. The distraught woman shared with her that she was trying to find Resurrection Downtown. The woman said, "I've been there before, but someone else was driving and I don't have my phone with me. I don't know where it is, and I really wanted to go to church tonight. I needed to be there tonight." The distraught woman asked her, "Do you know where it is?"

She replied and said, "Sure. I know where Resurrection Downtown is. Let's go there together." They walked and talked together until they eventually made it to the church—late but just in time for the sacrament of Holy Communion. As both of them stood in the entryway to the sanctuary, the young medical student paused to give her a hug and say good-bye, but the distraught woman was surprised and asked, "You're not staying? You should come in with me." The student said, "But I have places to go, a race to run, a workout to complete." The distraught woman urged her again saying, "You can do that later. Right now, you should come in with me..." So, she did.

They worshipped together, prayed together, and shared Communion with one another, and then after the worship service they shared with me why they were there and why this woman was distraught to begin with. This woman was distraught because she just done one of the most painful things a mother could ever do: she had signed away her parental rights, giving her daughter up for adoption. Living in the aftermath of this decision, this woman was looking for hope, life, and peace. Without knowing any of this, by God's grace, the fourth-year medical student made possible something extraordinary.

Out for a run, this young woman had a decision to make, and she chose to pursue the imperceptible. She was willing to see the things that most people overlook. She saw possibilities where others might not.

When I think about what God's Misfit Mission requires, I immediately think it requires openness to viewing interruptions as holy opportunities to do your best work. The Misfit Mission requires a mindset or a worldview that allows us to push past the predictable, familiar, and expected formulas and patterns that speak to efficiency and success and instead focus on the surprising and paradoxical rhythm of Christ's crazy life and unconditional love. God's Misfit Mission requires that we see possibilities even when others cannot.

Christ didn't see death; he saw opportunities for life. He didn't see darkness; he saw opportunities for light. He didn't see difference; he saw one body or the same spirit embedded within a diversity of unique gifts (cf. 1 Corinthians 12). He didn't see pain and suffering; he saw redemption and reconciliation. This is what we should see: possibilities abounding.

This vision should affect everything we do, including where we reside.

After we assembled a staff team and had a growing church community, we came to a point where we made the decision to purchase our first permanent space in downtown Kansas City. This decision was our biggest yet. After an extensive search we eventually landed on a former bar and concert venue named the Crosstown Station. Most people discouraged us from purchasing such a place, saying it was a mistake, it didn't fit our ethos, and they couldn't imagine a church holding worship services in a former bar. The Crosstown Station was an unconventional building to be sure, but, moreover, it was located smack dab in the middle of an unconventional neighborhood: an entertainment district filled with tattoo parlors, strip clubs, and nightclubs. Even though there were so many reasons to pass over this location, there was something undeniably right about it that we couldn't overlook. It had what we needed: a space to call our own in the middle of the city that came with parking. So, we ultimately pushed past our first impressions and closed on the property.

It took ten weeks to prepare the space before we opened the doors for our inaugural service the week before Christmas. The week leading up to our launch was filled with a flurry of activity. Some people spent time walking the neighborhood meeting our new neighbors. They walked in and out of all of the bars, restaurants, nightclubs, and even the strip clubs, dropping off Christmas poinsettias and invitations to join us in worship on Sunday morning. Their hope in going everywhere in our neighborhood was to build trust and rapport with our neighbors as well as invite them to join us. Some days they stayed out well past dark in order to do this.

At the same time, there was another group of people putting finishing touches on the building itself. They cleared out old equipment, emptied kegs, and filled dumpsters with the former bar's leftovers. They worked hard, doing whatever it took until the hour for launch was upon us. I joined them late on the Saturday night before we officially opened, and I had a moment to sit in the dark, looking out of the upstairs windows in what used to be a pool hall. This was my solitary moment of prayerful pause before things got crazy.

As I sat there, praying and looking out the windows at the downtown cityscape, I began seeing the neighborhood differently than I had before. I saw our neighbor to the north. Their business was called Temptations. Temptations is a strip club, and yet it is so much more. One can see the word *temptation* frequently in scripture. The word has scriptural allusions to the pathway that leads toward slavery to sin and death. Each week in worship we recite the words of the Lord's Prayer, "Lead me not into temptation, but deliver me from evil." So as I sat there, I thought to myself, "Head north and you have a scriptural allusion to hell or at least the pathway toward hell or evil."

Then I began looking to our neighbors to the south. The name of their business is the Mercy Seat. The Mercy Seat is a tattoo parlor in Kansas City, and yet it is so much more. The Mercy Seat is also something one can find in scripture. It describes the location where Moses delivered the law (cf. Exod 25:17). It is the location where God's word was read and proclaimed aloud. It denotes the place in ancient synagogues and temples where many believed heaven met earth.

The Mercy Seat, our neighbors to the south, was a scriptural allusion toward heaven or at least the pathway to heaven.

To the north we had temptations (hell), to the south we had the mercy seat (heaven), and our church was fixed firmly in between. That's when I remembered our building's former name. Our church was located in a bar formerly known as the Crosstown Station or, in church terms, "the Stations of the Cross." As I sat there, reflecting over all of this, everything was becoming crystal clear. I was beginning to see things that I missed upon first glance. Our church building was located exactly where it needed to be. The cross was positioned squarely in between heaven and hell. This was where hope would be born anew. This would be where death turns to life. This would be where light pierces the darkness.

As I sat pondering our church's location, positioned perfectly in between heaven and hell, I finally noticed the building located directly to our east, home to a local newspaper. It was all glass and it was built in such a way that it rose structurally toward the heart of city. At its highest point, illuminated for the entire city to see, was its name, the Kansas City Star. Not only were we precisely positioned between heaven and hell, but it came to my attention that we were also located squarely beneath "the Star" rising in the east. If ever there was a place to encounter the Christ child, it was here, but you had to have the eyes to see it. To most people, the Crosstown Station was simply an old rundown building that used to be a bar, but for our community this building was ripe with God's unlimited possibilities. It was a cradle of faith, hope, love, and life.

As we opened the church that December, we were in the midst of Advent. Advent comes from the Latin *adventus*, which translates as "arrival" or "what's coming." It is a season where we are filled with anticipation and great expectation awaiting the arrival of the coming one, Jesus Christ, Emmanuel, God-with-us.

In the middle of the night, as I sat in the church on the eve of our launch, it was clear that the glory of the Lord, this bright light, was shining all around us. In the same way that God spoke to the night-shift shepherds on Christmas, I felt the angel of the Lord speaking to me.

> "Don't be afraid! Look! I bring good news to you—wonderful, joyous news for all people. Your savior is born today in David's city. He is Christ the Lord. This is a sign for you: you will find a newborn baby wrapped snugly and lying in a manger." Suddenly a great assembly of the heavenly forces was with the angel praising God. They said, "Glory to God in heaven, and on earth peace among those whom he favors." (Luke 2:10-14)

And with this announcement, we all became recipients of a great and undeserved gift.

Upon receiving that gift in Luke, the shepherds responded by running with excitement from stable to stable with great expectation and smiles glorifying and praising God for all they had heard and seen, as it had been told them (Luke 2:15-20). They were God's Misfits in Mission. God's messengers who lived to tell others about the light and life of Christ.

So were we. We saw ourselves as being positioned in the right place at the right time and, in turn, God was calling us and commissioning us to tell others about our experience of God's perfect love in the center of the city. This was our mission. It was our mission back then on the night we first started, and it continues to be our mission to this day.

Discussion Questions

1. What do you see in the world around you? At work? At home? In the mission field?

2. Where do you need to push past your first glance in order to gaze upon God's presence?

3. What must you do in order to see, believe, and share eternal and unseen things with the world around you?

1. Henri J.M. Nouwen, *The Wounded Healer* (Garden City, NY: Doubleday, 1972), 75.

CHAPTER SIX

PRACTICE, PRACTICE, AND MORE PRACTICE MAKES PERFECT

A s I mentioned earlier, before I ever entertained thoughts of the ministry, my sole focus was Wall Street. My imagination was dominated by visions of a career that would one day take me to the trading floor of the New York Stock Exchange. I envisioned a lifetime of energy spent buying and selling stock while investing and accumulating large sums of money. Ministry wasn't on the radar.

Throughout my adolescence and in the early stages of my career, I believed with certainty that my life was built solely upon my ability and work ethic. If I was going to make it to Wall Street, then it would happen because I worked hard and nothing more. I was going to have to earn the success I desired. Needless to say, I was very driven to work. I was ready to do whatever it took to succeed. I wasn't ever going to take no for an answer.

During my first interview with my first investment company at the age of eighteen, I remember sharing these same kinds of thoughts with my future boss. Sitting in a boardroom, I said, "I promise you this: I will work hard for you and I am willing do whatever it takes in order to make it in this business, if only you'd give me the chance."

Upon hearing my promise, my future boss paused and took a good long look at me, a wet-behind-the-ears eighteen-year-old, standing five feet tall and wearing an oversized suit. Then, with a giant smile on his face, he chuckled, saying, "Scott, the investment world is nothing more than a big numbers game. If you're willing to play the numbers, then you'll make it. Focus on the numbers and you'll succeed. In fact, the first and only number you will ever need to know is three hundred. If you're willing to focus on that number, I'll hire you."

I responded, "Done. I love the number three hundred. It is my favorite number!" And it quickly became my favorite number. It was the first number I ever had to live into. Before I could make millions, get married, have children, retire, or golf, I needed to get through the number three hundred. My job required that I make three hundred phone calls every day, and if I was willing to actually make those three hundred dials to potential investors every day, I would eventually establish a base of clients that would allow me to succeed in business. It was as simple as that: a numbers game. Just smile and dial, and you'll succeed.

So I did. I made three hundred calls every day. Out of the three hundred phone calls I would typically engage in 150 actual conversations. Half of the people I called would be out of town, away from their phones, or perhaps intentionally screening my call. The other half of the people would actually answer. Those were what I considered to be actual conversations.

Then out of those 150 actual conversations, I generally experienced about seventy-five positive interactions. I defined a "positive interaction" as anything other than being hung up on or cursed out. Out of those seventy-five positive interactions I would then develop roughly thirty-five to forty prospects (or names of people who were open to further conversations and follow-up). These would eventually materialize into future phone calls with a specific purpose and real potential. They became my leads.

Out of those thirty-five to forty follow-up calls on leads, a little less than half would become hot leads. "Hot leads" were people who were looking to act fast and about half of them would eventually become clients.

If I haven't lost you yet, then you've certainly realized that if someone is willing to make three hundred phone calls a day, then they would eventually secure a grand total of eight to ten future clients. This is the numbers game. Three hundred phone calls = eight to ten clients. If someone wants to make a living or build a book of business, then all you would need to do is make three hundred phone calls every day. It is as simple as smiling and dialing and then you'll succeed.

When I started my career in investments, I made three hundred phone calls every day because that was the pathway toward success. So, I focused solely on the number three hundred. Everything else was insignificant. When I was making my calls, the response didn't matter. As people hung up on me or cursed me out (150 times daily) I simply pressed on, thinking, "You're one phone call closer to eight to ten. You're one call closer to your next yes." The numbers game made it so that things weren't emotional or personal. It was purely numerical. Three hundred phone calls equaled eight to ten new clients, plain and simple. No matter what happened on the other end of the line, I was able to continue working, knowing and trusting in the numbers.

When my wife and I settled down in Kansas City, we came with numerical expectations. We were expecting to be greeted by a large number of people who were excited about starting a church. In actuality, this number was much smaller. All in, there were nine of us.

We were a varied group based on any metric. We were extremely diverse in terms of gender, faith background, experience, age, and stage. We were misfits. We literally didn't fit together, nor was I sure that we belonged together. Some were studying to be doctors and some were salespeople. One was a CEO, another a CFO. There were a handful of other professionals as well. Nobody was the same. Nobody spoke each other's "language" or even lived in similar worlds. We were literally affinity-less.

The one thing that did bind us together was our focus on launching a new church. We wanted to build Christian community where nonreligious and nominally religious people could grow to become deeply committed Christians. We were bound together in our understanding that God was God, we were not, and more than anything, God longed for us to do the things that God did. We wanted to invite people to join us on this journey, but the question was "How?"

My instinct was to focus on the numbers by contacting as many people possible wherever we were, no matter what we were doing as often as possible. After all, this is what Jesus did.

In Luke 5, Jesus entered a new city. Once he arrived within the city limits, he immediately went to work meeting people. Everywhere he went, Jesus seemed to bump into people, heal people, redeem people, and invite people to join him. One day, Jesus even had the fortune of meeting a very specific kind of man, a man covered with leprosy.

The Levitical law toward lepers in Jesus's day allowed for all types of discrimination and prejudicial behavior by non-lepers toward the afflicted. First, the law required that a priest examine anyone suspected of leprosy. If the priest determined that the person had leprosy, he or she would be quarantined for seven days. At the end of the week's time, the priest could then either extend the quarantine another week or pronounce the person clean or, conversely, leprous.

If one had contracted leprosy, he or she was expelled from their communities, humiliated, and forced to out themselves or thereby demean themselves wherever they went. They were often relegated to the land just outside of the walls of the city into secluded enclaves or colonies. Lepers then (and in some cases still) literally became the outcast.

In Luke 5, as he enters into this new city, Jesus even meets one of these people.

> [Jesus] was in one of the cities, there was a man covered with leprosy. When he saw Jesus, he bowed with his face to the ground and begged him, "Lord, if you choose, you can make me clean." Then Jesus stretched out his hand, touched him, and said, "I do choose. Be made clean." Immediately the leprosy left him. And he ordered him to tell no one. "Go," he said, "and show yourself to the priest, and, as Moses commanded, make an offering for your cleansing, for a testimony to them." But now more than ever the word about Jesus spread abroad; many crowds would gather to hear him and to be cured of their diseases. (5:12-15 NRSV)

95

I love this story because it is so different than all the other healing stories. There are several stories of Jesus healing in scripture: the blind beggar, the man with the withered hand (Mark 3:1-6), Simon's mother-in-law (Mark 1:29-31), and the man beside the pool of Bethsaida (John 5). Almost everyone who came before Jesus was healed. But Jesus's healing in this case went beyond just physical ailments—it pressed into a social disease. Leprosy was also an accepted symbol for sin, separation, or isolation, which is something we all have experienced at some point in our lives. Sadly, it is something a lot of people have suffered at the hands of churches. So, Luke 5 reveals a story about Jesus venturing into a city, bumping into someone who didn't yet know God. Jesus did this always and everywhere he went.

Jesus was someone who gave himself to those whom he ministered. What started with the leper continued with the man born blind (John 9), the woman at the well (John 4), and the scores of sinners, tax collectors, and ne'er-do-wells. Jesus continuously gave himself to all of the misfits of the world and he invited them to join him in building Christian community. As we were beginning our journey to build Christian community in downtown Kansas City, God was inviting us to do the same thing.

This was fairly overwhelming in the beginning, so one of the first things we decided to do was set milestones or goals. We incorporated numbers into our journey of holy surprise. We used numbers not in terms of measuring people but in measuring our daily activity. Instead of focusing on the end, we focused on the means that would afford us God's desired end. In other words, we needed to focus on our practice. In order to do the things that God was calling us to do we needed to practice, practice, and practice some more. The Misfit Mission is a mission rooted in a measured and practical divinity. Practicing and measuring our practice would be essential to our success.

My favorite hockey player was a guy by the name of Wayne Gretzky. I liked him because he didn't fit into the NHL. He was small by outward appearance, but his God-given ability propelled him into superstardom, so much so that he was known as "the Great One." He was great because of his willingness to practice.

As I mentioned, Wayne Gretzky didn't possess the body of a hockey player. When he began his professional hockey career, he stood six feet tall and weighed in at 160 pounds. Wayne Gretzky was a misfit for the National Hockey League. Many critics claimed that he was too small, too wiry, and too slow to be a force in the NHL. But Wayne Gretzky had heart. He had drive. He had character and he had an unwavering desire to make the most of all that he'd been given, the power that he was born with. I guess you could say that he wanted to become the best version of the person God created him to be. So he practiced.

Wayne Gretzky had this vision. He believed that anyone could become an expert if they set aside enough time for practice. Malcolm Gladwell in his book *Outliers: The Story of Success* suggests, like Gretzky, that practice makes perfect. In fact, Gladwell said, "It only takes 10,000 hours."[1]

To become an expert, all that's required is that you play the numbers game, practice every day without fail until you reach ten thousand hours. So, for those of you who are doing the math already, in order to be an expert, this is what it takes:

- One hour per day requires 27 years, 139 days to become an expert.

- Two hours per day requires 13 years, 252 days to become an expert.

- Three hours per day requires 9 years, 46 days to become an expert.

- Four hours per day requires 6 years, 308 days to become an expert.

Are you willing to commit that consistent effort into becoming an expert? To fulfill your mission, purpose, or vision? Or to reflect God's image to the world around you? Are you willing to focus on the numbers and repetitions?

Wayne Gretzky contends that continuous practice is required in order to become great in hockey. Practice is also required as we journey down the pathway to God's perfect love as well. Love requires great practice, largely because loving one another is something we choose to do. Love is ultimately a decision we make and how loving we become is determined by our repetitive practice of it. Love is a practiced behavior whose depth is often measured by the quantity or frequency with which we demonstrate it.

John Wesley described our need to practice through his description of the tension felt between the form and power in our walk of faith. Finding a balance between form and power, Wesley argued, was key to living fully in light of who God is and who God created us to be.

Whenever Wesley used the word *power,* he was referring to our experience of the Holy Spirit. God's Spirit leads us with power and grace, with spontaneity and unmistakable force. It interrupts our daily life as it pleases in ways that warm our hearts, and it moves in and through all things. For Wesley, God's Spirit was all-powerful and ever-present throughout all of creation; this was the "power" that Wesley most often referred to in our walk of faith. This power was the surprising force behind his conversion at Aldersgate Street. However, one's walk of faith required more than just power. It also demanded *form*.

For Wesley, "form" was simply a way of referring to the structures and systems that we place around the free-flowing movement of God's Holy Spirit as it works its way throughout all of creation. Wesley's structures often looked like measures, or systems of accountability, rules of order or discipline. These "forms" or measures helped Wesley and the people called Methodists to harness the Holy Spirit's power in ways that focused it in one single direction, into a movement or collective.

As we gathered together to do the things that God does in downtown Kansas City, we needed to have the power and freedom to go wherever the Spirit led us. We needed to maintain openness toward God's holy interruptions always and everywhere. However, simply following wherever the Spirit led us without purpose or focus wouldn't have helped us accomplish our mission. It would have left us feeling tossed about like a feather in the wind.

Think about the destruction potential of tornadoes and hurricanes. Wind moving in a focused direction can be deadly. However, if the breeze were to simply blow where it may, it loses all of its life-changing power and awe. The Misfit Mission of building community and changing lives requires more than just power or form. It requires a tension between the two. It requires form and power or, more specifically, God's power and our corresponding practice.

John Wesley and his mission with the people called Methodists was Spirit-driven and faithfully practiced. Wesley's attention to both form and power enabled his movement of misfits to both recognize and respond to the spontaneous interruptions of the Holy Spirit, or God's definitive call. They were able to do this largely because they had honed their method or practice. They were living out a disciplined and measured faith. Their practical divinity ultimately shaped and enflamed the world around them, birthing more than just a church, but also orphanages, hospitals, lending institutions, soup kitchens, and universities among other things. Our mission must be structured in the same way.

As Resurrection Downtown was forming, we were diligent in our attentiveness to the movement of the Holy Spirit and sought always to respond to its leading with measured discipline, effort, and persistence. In order to become the community God was calling us to be, we employed our gifts repetitively, in a practiced fashion, so that we would be able to experience the greater things God was calling and equipping us to do, namely to change the world. In order to live fully into God's Misfit Mission, we had to be willing to do whatever it takes while always paying close attention to the numbers.

God's Misfit Mission requires daily discipline and practice. It is defined by the movement of the Holy Spirit and our persistent corresponding response of love. We must practice, practice, and practice some more. We must be willing to play the numbers game.

Are you practicing?

Are you smiling and dialing?

In order to live fully into the mission God has for us, we need to focus our response and efforts in a measurable way. If we open ourselves to the movement of the Spirit and then seek to measure our activity in quantifiable ways, then we can strive for perfection by improving our ability to reflect God's image to the world around us according to God's grace because everything we do would be measured and held accountable.

We need to practice, but that requires we first figure out what our primary practice and measure should be. That's what we had to determine next.

Discussion Questions

1. How do you measure your life? Success?

2. What are your Christian practices for becoming the best version of the person God created you to be?

3. How are you becoming an instrument of God's peace for the world around you?

4. How are you harnessing God's Spirit and power?

1. Malcom Gladwell, *Outliers: The Story of Success* (New York: Little, Brown and Company, 2008).

CHAPTER SEVEN

GETTING OUT INTO THE MISSION FIELD: A TALE OF THIRTY-FIVE PENNIES AND A LOT OF WATER

At the end of the last chapter I asked you to consider how you measure your life, and I pushed you toward the importance of personal practices, but what are the primary ways we should respond to God's call or the movement of the Holy Spirit in order to change the world?

Chen Si is a man who lives in the shadow of the Yangtze River Bridge in China, the Nanjing, Jiangsu Province. Every day he employs the practice of walking across his neighborhood bridge (which just so happens to be huge, measuring 525 ft in height and 5171 ft in length).[1] Chen's neighborhood bridge carries approximately eighty thousand vehicles and two hundred trains per day. It is also interesting to note that this bridge is also the most popular suicide site in the world. Knowing this, Chen Si, in his off time, walks and watches for other pedestrians who happen to walk across this bridge. In his daily practice of walking, over the past decade, it has been estimated that he has saved more than two hundred people who tried to end their lives by jumping off the bridge. Walking the same bridge every day with repetition and purpose has made new life possible in a place marred by death.

What compels Chen to do this?

Earlier in his life Chen Si suffered the loss of a close relative at the hands of suicide and it made him wonder what would happen if someone were willing to lend a hand to another at that critical moment of being surrounded by the darkness of death. So Chen now lives a life that tries to answer that question. He tries to be there for people. He walks back and forth over the bridge, looking to meet people, to bump into them during their moments of darkness with a word, a hand, a hotel room, counseling referrals, and with everything and anything else he has. He has saved more than two hundred people. Can you believe this? Something as simple as walking a bridge on a daily basis has the capacity to change lives by the grace of Jesus Christ.

Chen has become a hero, one of God's Misfits in Mission, a reflection of God's image to the world around him in ways that changes lives and transforms the world. Chen's mission is rooted in daily practice and through that practice Chen's survivors have experienced the life that really is life. What's more is that many have returned to join him in this daily practice of bridge walking, hoping to share the same life with others. Chen Si is not only changing lives, but he is transforming an entire community that longs to do the same thing.

Michael Wheeler is a man who doesn't walk across bridges but rather runs through the streets of Kansas City wearing a Superman costume. People call him "the Superman of Midtown."[2] His daily practice is to run throughout the city hoping to share inspiration and hope. He's a running evangelist, seeking to share the good news of Jesus Christ with everyone he meets, and in order to start conversations with the strangers on the street, he wears a Superman costume. His costume, combined with his willingness and determination to meet people where they are, conjures up all kinds of positive encounters. Michael meets and inspires dozens of people on a daily basis in a way that lifts the hearts and minds of all of those around him simply by engaging others in positive, uplifting, and life-giving conversation and surprise.

Maybe running in costume isn't your practice or maybe you have a fear of walking across bridges, but you can definitely do something. Can you read the newspaper?

A couple of years ago, friends of mine suffered one of the worst losses imaginable. They had lost their child in the midst of tragic circumstances. Their world had been turned upside down. "Parents aren't supposed to outlive their children," they shared with me, and yet this was now their reality. They were left in the darkness, stuck and wondering what to do. In those dark days, the strangest thing happened. An anonymous note arrived in the mail. Not knowing what it might be or who it could be from, they opened it.

Inside it read,

> Two years ago, my pastor said that everyone has some practice, some discipline, some gift that they can offer to change the world and this just so happens to be mine. Everyday I look through the obituaries and I look for families of military men and women, and I send them anonymous letters to offer them hope in the midst of despair, light in the midst of darkness and life in the midst of death. I want you to know that you aren't alone. I am here with you and so is God.

Upon opening this letter, my friends were inspired by the grace of this great gift and practice. They experienced a reminder of God's life that dances even in the midst of darkness and death.

What is your practice? How is God calling you into mission?

These were the questions I posed to our band of misfits at Resurrection Downtown as we went to work starting our church. What should we do? How should we measure our efforts? How could we practice our faith and live into God's Misfit Mission?

We each have something we can do in order to meet people where they are. God calls and equips each of us uniquely to do the things that God does, which means that we all have a part to play. Each and every one of us has passions, unique gifts, and the capacity to change the world by the grace of Jesus Christ. Maybe it looks like walking the same bridge with eyes that search for people in crisis previously unseen. Maybe it looks like reading the obituaries each day with eyes fixed on seeing people in need of surprising hope in the midst of darkness and death. Maybe it is something else.

My preferred practice involves ingesting caffeine. God has called and equipped me with the unique ability to drink large amounts of coffee, and meet people in coffee shops. This is how I live fully into the mission God has for me.

I love getting to know my neighbors. I get to know them by doing the normal neighborly type of activities. I walk my dog and exchange greetings. On snowy days, I scrape their car windshields and shovel sidewalks. I carry groceries, hold open doors, get the mail, and watch their pets, but none of that is what really sets me apart or gets me excited. For me, in order to fulfill the call God has placed on my heart, I like to venture beyond the convention of normal neighborly stuff. I like to get out there. I like to be synchronized with the flow and rhythm of the neighborhood. I like to walk around in it, explore it, live in it, and experience the very best and worst of it. In downtown Kansas City, and for me personally, the starting point for doing this is to visit all the local coffee shops.

Coffee shops are sought-after gathering spaces. They are the places where locals hang out in the hopes of connecting with one another. The people who go to coffee shops are almost always people looking for a connection. You'll see people tirelessly working on their laptops (even on weekends), but they aren't really working at their full potential. Why are they there? I believe it is largely to avoid the deafening silence and isolation of working from home.

In coffee shops you will find lots of people reading books, not necessarily because it's the place to get quality reading done, but because the coffee shop provides them with a place to be seen, to be social, to build community, and find life— maybe even life with a new friend who enjoys the same author or the same kinds of books.

In coffee shops you will also find tables filled with old friends talking with one another, often not so they could have the deep and meaningful conversation reserved for intimate friends, but so that two friends can enjoy the simple comforts of fellowship all around them while catching up on life, events, and the latest gossip.

Additionally, coffee shops are filled with baristas who often work in coffee shops so that they can have great conversations with unique people (maybe even pastors) all day long. Baristas are often incredible conversationalists. Coffee shops are filled with people who want to be surrounded by others even when they don't have to be. Coffee shop patrons are people who want to be seen, interrupted, or distracted. They want to be a part of the broader community.

I learned this by drinking massive amounts of coffee and having hundreds, if not thousands, of conversations.

As I set out to do the things that Jesus did, meet people where they are as they are, I focused on meeting the most people possible. During my first thirty-one days in Kansas City, I went to thirty-three coffee shops, and I set a numerical goal for each visit. Instead of making three hundred dials every day, my goal was to bump into, meet, and invite thirty-five people a day to join me in building Christian community in downtown Kansas City. As a way of holding myself accountable to the numbers, I carried thirty-five pennies around with me everywhere I went.

Each morning when I woke up, I placed thirty-five pennies in the front right pocket of my pants, and throughout the day I hoped to initiate thirty-five corresponding conversations that would eventually lead people to the church. For each such conversation (that led to the church) I moved a single penny from my right pocket to my left. My practice was to not return home until all thirty-five pennies made it into my left pocket.

These conversations often began with small talk and then transitioned into a conversation that eventually pointed toward the church. I would ask a question pertaining to that particular stranger's occupation or vocation, hoping that, if asked, the question would be reciprocated so that I could have an opportunity to share the details of what I was doing in Kansas City, namely building Christian community in downtown Kansas City. Once a conversation had fully transitioned to the point that I shared the story of Resurrection Downtown and exchanged my business card with the other person, I would then move the penny from my right pocket to the left pocket.

Since we started Resurrection Downtown, people have asked me, "How did you manage all of these conversations? It seems like you would have needed some sort of strategy to accomplish this level of interaction."

As I set out to bump into my neighbors and meet them where they were, it got to the point that I needed a plan for when and where these conversations would take place in the community coffee shops. Here are some of the strategies I focused on when approaching each coffee shop so as to maximize opportunities for conversation. (Incidentally, all of this also translates to small diners, local watering holes, wherever you find God placing you.)

Strategies for Maximizing Coffee Shop Conversations

- Wait to enter the coffee shop until a line has formed.

- Get in line (and never cut in line, as that will initiate a conversation with a different tenor).

- Initiate conversation with the person standing in front of you in line.

- Next, engage the barista in conversation at the counter while ordering coffee.

- Always order a drink that requires time and preparation (Americanos are best if you like black coffee and are on a budget).

- Introduce yourself to the barista and talk long enough until the person behind you in line steps up to order.

- Introduce that person (the one behind you in line) to the barista you just met and to yourself.

- While waiting for your Americano, talk to the person behind you in line, and ask about their drink.

- Before leaving, take fifteen minutes to sit and survey the coffee shop. Look for people reading familiar books, sitting by themselves, or typing by themselves, and sit near them.

I would talk to an average of three to five people about our new church in every coffee shop I entered. About half of my conversations went really well. After telling people that I was a new pastor of a new church, some would engage me with all sorts of exciting questions. They would want to know about our vision, our purpose, or our mission. They would ask me about service opportunities and worship times.

Admittedly, though, not everybody enjoyed meeting the new pastor in town. About half of the conversations I entered into weren't at all well received. Some were very awkward. In these instances, upon learning that I was a pastor at a new church, these people would generally tell me about how they used to go to church when they were in the third grade, or how they didn't believe in God at all, or that they simply weren't interested. It would have been easy to get discouraged by those conversations, and at times I was. However, what I noticed over time was that even though conversations didn't go well, the simple act of having a conversation with a pastor at a coffee shop was enough to leave a lasting impact. Sometimes even then my conversation made a difference.

As I later found out, sometimes these disinterested people would go on to talk with a friend, a spouse, or a co-worker later in the day. During those subsequent conversations, they would be asked about their day, and almost always they would share the surprising news that they had had a cup of coffee with "a new pastor in town."

This would shock their friend, spouse, or whomever they were talking to. And that would elicit some response like, "Since when are you the type of person who would have coffee with a pastor?"

This kind of question would then inevitably trigger some type of defensive retort like, "Since when am I *not* the kind of person who would talk with a pastor?! I can talk with a pastor if I want to!" And usually, in a matter of moments, the person who didn't like me at first was now on my team, defending our conversation. Over the course of the past five years, there have been several instances where people were excited about sharing with their friends and family that they had a conversation with me, largely because this kind of activity was surprising interruption into their everyday routine. My coffee shop conversations were holy surprises largely because most people aren't willing or looking to have conversations with strangers, and most pastors aren't willing to engage people where they are and as they are. All of this combined made my coffee shop experiences even better because, in time, I couldn't go anywhere without bumping into someone who remembered me or who had heard a reference to me. In fact, most people were actually excited to see me or excited that I remembered them when we bumped into each other a second or third time.

Now, of course, there were some really tough conversations too. Sometimes I wonder what would have happened had I focused on those conversations as I sometimes did in my former investment world. Sometimes I wonder what might have happened if I focused on the elements of the negative conversations instead of focusing on the measured practice of meeting a daily numerical goal. In the same way, I wonder what would have happened if Jesus had focused on the negative social implications of talking with the lepers or dining with tax collectors and sinners.

Even Jesus worked the numbers. Jesus was disciplined in his practice of selfless and sacrificial love in his mission to change lives and transform the world. Jesus focused on the meeting as many people possible always and everywhere. He focused on the frequency of interactions with the world around him. Nothing was going to stop him. Jesus was going to keep on bumping into people, touching them, healing them, and inviting them to go and do likewise. Everywhere he went he sought out interactions, conversations, loving embraces, and healing words. He paid attention to the numbers too! The Gospels record that he fed four thousand people right here (Matt 15:32-39) and another five thousand people over there (John 6:1-15). He talked about the faith of *the four* friends here (Luke 5:17-25), and focused on the ministry of *the twelve* disciples there. The Gospels were always referring to the numbers of encounters, conversations, and personal touches that Jesus's Misfit Mission was amassing, and even Jesus applied numerical measures to how and how frequently we ought to forgive one another: "not

just seven times, but rather as many as seventy-seven times"
(Matt 18:22).

For the first twelve months of being in KC, I immersed
myself in the practiced discipline of meeting as many people
as possible so that I might experience and become part of
the rhythm and beauty of this eclectic community with all
the energy I could muster and all the focus I could apply. I
journeyed out into the community with every opportunity
I had to meet people where they were. And it was fun. (It is
still fun!)

In my comings and goings and through my coffee shop
conversations, I have discovered great places to taste, see,
and experience the best our community has to offer. I also
discovered a quiet but discernible disconnect amongst most
of the people I spoke with. There were so many great people
doing so many great things, but there wasn't an overriding
sense of community at all. I met with a bunch of individuals; in fact, I was living in a building full of them. However, there wasn't a clear sense of togetherness or oneness.
There was no cross-conversation, nobody pulling together,
no community, and yet many of the people I met with had
a pronounced desire to become a part of something bigger.
They wanted connection.

Visiting coffee shops is my practice, but it wasn't going to be everybody's. As Resurrection Downtown began, I
turned toward the other nine misfits in our fledgling community and invited them to consider what their practice was
going to be. How was God calling and equipping them to
meet as many people as they could in the hopes of building
community and changing lives?

Among the nine, there was a couple who was creative and artistic by nature. As a part of their efforts, they sought out opportunities to meet up with people in their circles of influence in some of the more creative neighborhoods within the city. They purchased pallets of bottled water, put them into coolers, and camped out in front of art galleries and music venues in order meet their neighbors by giving them a free gift (a cold bottle of water on a hot day). As they handed out the water, they had conversations and eventually shared stories of the church with people who lived and moved and had their being within the creative arts community.

There was another couple who liked riding bikes, so they did something similar. They purchased water as well, and set up water stations all throughout the community at races and on courses that allowed for them to be present at finish lines, celebrating with their neighbors over a congratulatory bottle of water. What happened over time was that whenever someone crossed the finish line or stopped at a water station, they were able to have a surprising conversation about the church. This couple also made sure they rode their bikes in as many races, charity rides, and casual bike groups as they could with eyes fixed on meeting and befriending others.

As the church began to grow, we also had people doing similar things in bars, restaurants, offices, and apartment buildings. Everywhere that there were people, our misfits were bound together in mission, seeking to meet as many people as possible in ways that befriended, loved, and invited others in the same way that Jesus befriended, loved, and invited us. This is the Misfit Mission in motion.

In the Gospels, Jesus reminds us that we are all called and commissioned to make disciples of all nations, baptizing them in the name of the Father, Son, and Holy Spirit so that we might transform the world (Matt 28:19). Disciples are people who follow and live in the pattern and pathway of another. In Christian circles, to be a disciple is to be a follower of the path that Christ sets. It's a path that leads toward redemption, toward resurrection, toward life that really is life. It's a path that makes possible the reflection of God's image displayed for the entire world to see.

The Misfit Mission is a pathway that serves to bind people together by weaving our own creative threads or affinities together in a way that produces a coherent tapestry with the power and potential to cover an entire city in God's grace and glory.

Put simply, following God's Misfit Mission or Christ's path is striving to live in a way that serves others and loves others the way that Christ first loved us so that together we might experience God's kingdom here on earth just as it is in heaven.

After fifty-three days, our band of misfits that numbered nine had transformed into a community of about seventy-five people. After three months of this same practiced discipline, we numbered over two hundred. To think that in such short time this band of misfits had multiplied in mission from nine individuals into a community of two hundred was pretty astonishing. Then again it became another moment for us to remember that by the grace given us and through the discipline of doing whatever it takes, with a focus on numbers, greater things were yet to come and greater things were still to be done in our mission field.

After three months of this, we wondered and imagined together asking, "What would happen if we continued reaching out like this with the love of Christ everywhere we went, in order to invite all of the misfits living, moving, and dreaming in downtown Kansas City to build community and to collaborate with us? How might this city look different because of it?"

Discussion Questions

1. What is your daily practice?

2. What are you doing regularly in order to become the best version of the person you were created to be and to transform the world around you?

3. How are you measuring your activity?

1. Liang Chen, "Man devotes life to thwarting suicide attempts, rehabilitating," *Global Times*, April 19, 2013, www.globaltimes.cn/content/776210.shtml.

2. Elana Gordon, "Getting to Know Midtown's 'Running Superman,'" KCUR 89.3, May 13, 1013, http://kcur.org/post/getting-know-midtowns-running-superman.

CHAPTER EIGHT

THE POWER OF WORDS

A s this community of misfits at Resurrection Downtown ventured into the community, meeting our neighbors and engaging strangers in holy and surprising conversation, one thing we quickly realized was that our words mattered. What we said would oftentimes leave a lasting impression.

When Jesus healed the leper in Luke 5 he used very specific words. He healed with the word *katharizō* (an ancient Greek word meaning forgiveness). Jesus used this word to intentionally point us toward the man's spiritual condition as opposed to physical ailment. Similarly, when Jesus healed the man lying by the pool of Bethesaida, he told the man, "Get up! Pick up your mat and walk" (John 5:8). These words spoke to the man's stuck condition, not his physical infirmity. God's Misfit Mission is similarly rooted in very specific words, and this is good news because the words that we share with others have real power. Our conversations with others can be life changing.

Our. Words. Have. Power.

Words have the ability to leave a residue that many of us will carry around for our entire lives. I will never forget that moment when my wife Wendy said, "Yes!" when I asked her to marry me. I'm still not sure she knew what she was getting herself into, but when she said that one simple single syllable word, it changed my life. That was a word that I will never forget.

Equally, I'll never forget hearing the words, "Congratulations, you're having a baby!" I'm still not quite sure what all of fatherhood entails, but I'm pretty sure those words have changed my life forever.

There are other words I carry with me as well. I'll never forget when I got the call where the other voice on the phone said, "Scott, I'm so sorry but she's gone. Your grandmother has passed away" or "Unfortunately, corporate has decided to make some cuts" or, even worse, "I'm afraid there's nothing more we can do."

Words have power. They shape us. Impact us. Change us. Some words encourage us and others discourage us. The author of Proverbs writes,

> Death and life are in the power of the tongue. (Prov 18:21)

And in James we read,

> With [the tongue] we both bless the Lord and Father and curse human beings made in God's likeness. Blessing and cursing come from the same mouth. (Jas 3:9-10)

Words can do other sorts of things as well. They have the power to surprise us and confound us. They can bless us and curse us. They can also soothe us with a familiar comfort. This is what I love about Christmas.

Christmas (or the season of Advent within the church) is one of my favorite seasons of the year, not because of the lights or the presents, but because it is a season filled with familiar words. During Christmas, the weary world rejoices in familiar words, and it feels good. It's comfortable. It makes it the most wonderful time of the year. People can be standing in line waiting to purchase presents and the whole time familiar Christmas carols filter down like snow upon the entire experience, and everyone is happy and bright. The same is true whenever we turn on the TV. At Christmas, every other channel we click on has one of those familiar movies or television specials that we grew up watching and we can't get enough of them. *A Christmas Story* runs for twenty-four hours straight, and so does *Home Alone* and *National Lampoon's Christmas Vacation*. There's more too. We go to school auditoriums to watch our kids dress up and sing the same songs. We go out with friends and family to see the same familiar plays and musicals. We identify with all the characters. We know all of the lines. We have the entire story imprinted upon our hearts and it is everywhere we go. And this doesn't just apply to people in the church. This also applies to everybody.

In one of my ongoing attempts to meet with people where they are, I regularly travel beyond the local coffee shop to a local bar on Wednesday nights to play trivia. On a Wednesday in December, one of the categories was "Christmas Movie Lines." The host played audio clips from famous Christmas movies and the trivia teams listened to the clip and made their guess as to which movie the clip came from.

On that particular evening, every team in the bar managed to answer every question correctly. However, the most impactful was when the last audio clip came from the scene where Linus (from *A Charlie Brown Christmas*) recites the

Christmas story as recorded in the second chapter of Luke. As the audio clip began to play, I sat back and watched as the entire bar listened intently to the recitation of scripture over the loudspeaker, and what was even more powerful was that each team knew the story word for word. In fact, most actually began to join in with Linus. This is Christmas and this is the power of words. They stick with us, and in this case, they become imprinted upon our hearts. The words at Christmas become a part of our flesh. The word became flesh in the bar that night, and I still get chills thinking about it. Words have power.

The Gospel of John doesn't let us forget the power of words. John reminds us of their power by taking us all the way back to the beginning of time. According to John, Jesus's story (the Christmas story) doesn't begin in a manger with angels and shepherds; it starts well before any of those things. Jesus's story in John begins with echoes of the words written in Genesis. John starts the story by saying, "In the beginning..." (John 1:1).

John doesn't start out saying "Once upon a time..." Instead he says, "Once, before time ever was..." The Gospel of John forcibly reorients us. It changes our perspective. It takes us back before time, saying, "In the beginning, before there was anything else, including time, Jesus *was.*"

> In the beginning was the Word and the Word was with God and the Word was God. (John 1:1)

John says Jesus was *this* Word. He was the Word with God that was in the beginning, speaking all of creation into being. John jogs our memory of a familiar Christmas story by reminding us about how in the very beginning, God used words to create the world and everything in it. God's words are powerful. They bring forth light and life.

God said, "Let there be light." And so light appeared. (Gen 1:3)

In the beginning, God used words rhythmically and repetitively, like verses in a song, to bring about life. Over and over again, God speaks and life emerges and nothing can stop it. John begins the Christmas story the very same way and in so doing pushes us past the predictable in order to capture the mystery, wonder, and power of the Word of God resting beneath the surface—if only we had the eyes to see it and believe it.

The Gospel of John spares us all the plotlines, genealogical accounts, or chronological details and instead composes one of the most beautiful songs of praise, celebrating the fact that the God of the Universe is coming into the picture once again. John's words tell the story of what Charles Wesley referred to as the second birth of all creation, and it does not begin in a manger. It begins in the beginning. John's words help us to find new life even in the familiar story. His words become a holy surprise that confront us by saying, "Don't miss the power behind this word." And then in one sentence, John reminds us that **this same word becomes like us.** "The Word became flesh and made his home among us. We have seen his glory, glory like that of a father's only son, full of grace and truth" (John 1:14).

The Word became flesh and lived among us. The Word that was with God in the beginning speaking light and life into the darkness has become like us. It lives among us. It is embodied. The life-giving Word of God has changed form and shape. The message has become the messenger. The word now has a pair of legs and is able to bump into us wherever we are with light, life, and unconditional love. God changes the game at Christmas and compels us to do the same.

This is God's promise for us at Christmas: the Word of the Lord is no longer simply a message restricted to the pages of scripture, sheets of music, or even the familiar movies and television programs we watch hours on end. The Word is enfleshed. We are called to go and do likewise, to do the things that God does, to be like Christ. So go therefore and let your light shine before others that they might see your good works, and give glory to God in heaven, because of what they have seen in you (cf. Matt 5:16). This is God's Misfit Mission. This is our mission and it comes through our living words. **Your life is the only scripture that most people will ever read. By your words spoken and enacted, you become the word of God that others will experience.**

Are your words communicating the light and life of Christ? How are you giving the story legs with your words or with your life?

To be one of God's Misfits is to take up the way of the Word made flesh, and to commit ourselves to living and sharing the ongoing message of Christ. Each of us must become the Word of God spoken and embodied for our workplaces, neighborhoods, families, and friends. God chooses us. God calls us and has equipped us to express some aspect of the divine word through our lives.

The fundamental questions following our decisions of personal disciplines and practices aimed at reaching out to the mission field as Resurrection Downtown were the questions of what and how we would communicate. I asked the earliest members of our young church, "What message are you communicating in both word and deed?" and "How are you living out the powerful words of God's promise and hope to the weary world around you?"

I wondered about this constantly and I urged our community to pay continual attention not only to our actions and physical presence in the mission field (coffee shops, races, community events), but to our vocabulary as well, because words have power.

As members of the launch team continuously sought to meet people in the mission field, we began uncovering some sweeping themes. A majority of the people we were meeting during our initial efforts exhibited a great degree of criticism toward Christianity and specifically churches themselves (the very thing we wanted to build). There was a marked sense of disengagement and disillusionment. Many were skeptical, feeling the church was too rigid, full of hypocrites, antihomosexuality, and altogether problematic due to its overinvolvement in American politics. Additionally, there seemed to be a level of institutional distrust with its leaders.

After listening to enough people, our launch team started to feel the need to put together an intentional plan of approach and specific communication that accompanied our practice. We not only vowed to pay careful attention to the words we used whenever we engaged in these conversations, but our physical presence needed to speak just as loudly. If we were to effectively communicate and share the love of God, we needed to first establish trust rooted in unconditional love.

123

Step One: Be Present

One of the ways we established trust was by simply becoming dependable and reliable. We attempted to be present wherever people were. We just wanted to bump into people, the same way that the Word made flesh bumped into us, and not just at the coffee shops, but at the grocery store, in art galleries, on the bike path, at restaurants—literally everywhere people were. Being present with the community around us fostered trust and made possible the formation of authentic relationships rooted in proximity, geography, and shared affinity. Being present is our practice and is perhaps the most significant component to doing the things that Jesus did.

Step Two: Imagine Your Words as ARMs

Next, as we focused on being present where we were planted, we imagined our words as arms: articulate, apologetic, relevant, relational, and missional (ARMs).

If we were going to reach people with our words we needed to be **Articulate** and **Apologetic** in ways that could disarm skepticism. This didn't mean that we went around saying "I'm sorry" to everybody we encountered, but we sought to be apologetic in ways that communicated matters of the faith articulately. We needed to be able to defend our faith articulately and authentically, especially in the face of tough questions. Being ill-prepared with phrases like "Everything happens for a reason," or "This is just a part of God's plan," or "The Bible says it. I believe it. That settles it" wouldn't suffice. The people we typically met and the lives they were living were far too complicated for the simplicity of these pithy sayings. This kind of communicating was unacceptable. Instead, we attempted to always offer a rational and humble defense of the faith as we knew it, personally. We sought to explain why we believed what we believed, why we lived the way we lived, and why our lives were fundamentally different because of our faith.

In order to build trust and reach the people we didn't know (who were already skeptical of the church) we needed to be able to articulate a response for tough questions without settling for easy half answers, which, of course, implied that we had to be comfortable saying "I don't know."

So many people try to teach, solve, or find easy answers to complex questions. That was not Resurrection Downtown. We sought always to articulate our faith using personal apologetics, beginning first with our own experience as to why Christ is important to us. If we hadn't experienced it, thought about it, or ever tried to understand it, we simply had to say, "I don't know. What do you think?" This is oftentimes how Jesus spoke when confronted with questions.

Whenever pressed with questions, rather than answering definitively, Jesus almost always replied with additional questions. He always continued the conversation. In Luke 10, a legal expert asked Jesus, "What must I do to gain eternal life?" Rather than answering, Jesus replied by asking, "What is written in the Law? How do you interpret it?" (Luke 10:25-28).

When Jesus healed the man with the withered hand in the temple on the Sabbath, Jesus was questioned as to why he chose to heal on the Sabbath. Rather than answering, Jesus replied with another question: "Here's a question for you: Is it legal on the Sabbath to do good or to do evil, to save life or to destroy it?" (Luke 6:9). In other words, Jesus asked the Pharisees questions in response to their question. Jesus rarely answered but instead called for others' opinions: "Is the Sabbath intended to give life or take it away? Would it be better that this man should die or that I heal him? You tell me."

The Word of God never settled for easy answers, and neither should we. As a way of equipping our launch team we prepared by reading books together and invited others to join us as well. We read *Seeing Gray in a World of Black and White* by Adam Hamilton and *The Reason for God: Belief in an Age of Skepticism* by Tim Keller.[1] This would give us some comfort in that we could simply invite anyone we met who had specific questions to read these books with us as a way of starting and/or continuing the conversation, as opposed to offering any overly simplistic answers to tough and oftentimes loaded questions. Reading books together and engaging in thoughtful dialogue and research is almost always the best way forward. So this was how we best articulated our faith and helped others to do the same authentically and apologetically.

In addition to being apologetic and articulate, we also realized that in order for our words to become like arms, we had to be **Relevant** or **Relational.** Whenever we were talking with strangers, we needed to be comfortable using creative mediums and metaphors commonly associated with emerging trends and social mediums. We engaged the culture around us, seeking to speak in languages others could understand. In addition to face-to-face conversations, we engaged social media by creating accounts on Instagram, Facebook, and Twitter. We reduced almost all things down to bite-sized bits of sound and story in order to provoke imagination and wonder. We learned how to speak with raw images and unedited videos using a wide variety of hashtags and memes. We shied away from anything overly polished. In doing so, we left room for mistaken wonder, varied interpretation, and ongoing conversations. We saw this as being similar to the way Jesus used parables in order to convey his messages of grace and truth. People in Jesus's day and age understood stories, and they learned through overarching narrative metaphors and figures of speech. And so the result was that many of Jesus's teachings were contained in parables or the stories of scripture. In the same way, we realized that we were living within the world of YouTube stories, Vine videos, Twitter feeds, and Instagram streams. So we decided that we needed to be there, speaking in those mediums as well. In fact, some of our earliest community gatherings were initiated on Facebook, and we continue to push people to those spaces where people can engage in conversation without overstepping their personal comfort levels or barriers.

Learning how to speak in these ways allowed for sweeping influence in a short period of time. Entering into conversations on Twitter, Instagram, and Facebook makes possible connections that no coffee shop could ever facilitate. In fact, conversations online often provoked a sweeping response, complete with more rough edges, tough questions, and provocative thought in newsfeeds and the comment sections than one could ever think to ask or imagine.

In and through all of these conversations, we quickly realized that talk is cheap when it only involves our words—verbal or virtual. Being present in the comment section is different than walking through something and actually getting your hands dirty. We felt a deep and urgent need to move all of our conversations into action. We need not simply learn how to talk the talk, but we needed to walk the talk as well. Our messages needed to invite or invoke opportunities for becoming messengers.

If our words were to become arms, we needed to them to be **Missional,** intentionally set on leading people into opportunities where together we could get our hands dirty in the business of changing the world. Our conversations and questions should always seek to lead others into acts of service. This was also a tactic Jesus employed. If Jesus could have branded it, I suspect he would have called it his "Come and See" strategy for inviting people into a life of faith or into an experience of the Holy Spirit.

"Don't believe me? Well, come and see," said Jesus.

Jesus invited his disciples saying, "Come, follow me, and I'll show you how to fish for people" (Mark 1:17). So, too, should our words always seek to invite people to join us in action. Every Saturday morning we hosted get-togethers at various social services throughout the mission field, with the hopes that all throughout the week, people could extend invitations to their conversation partners saying, "Come and see what we're up to this Saturday." Time and time again, people would join us to serve one another, to experience the life-giving power and joy of sacrifice and service.

Our vision was to transform the city (resurrect downtown) authentically, creatively, and passionately by the grace of Jesus Christ using the words in **ARMs**—outstretched and hoping to speak to all those around us in ways that invite new life and pathways forward. Through the power of words, people from all different segments of the community have joined us in our mission. We have a surplus of young professionals and millennial men and women between the ages of eighteen and thirty-five. They constitute roughly half of our congregation. This is the misfit generation if there ever was one within the church.

We've also experienced lots of artists gravitating back toward our emerging faith community. As a way of speaking with them, we needed to learn an entirely new language, one that didn't involve words, only freedom of expression and interpretation. We took the exterior wall of our church building (the converted bar) and transformed it into a blank canvas. We put out a "request for proposal" as a way of inviting the most creative people in the city to display on the side of our building what "resurrection downtown" looked like to them. Through our request for proposal we were inviting them to show their creative understanding of the importance of resurrection within our community. That was met with such overwhelming interest that we opened up our sanctuary walls that they too might become a gallery of modern day, stained glass, inspired works by local artists for our church and city.

Every month a new artist from the broader community now hangs his or her artwork for display inside our sanctuary as a part of our worship space and experience. Worship has literally become a place where every month people from the community share some of the most amazing fabric, oil, print, and photography art with our faith community as an act of worship. Everyone who enters the space can experience God in worship in beautiful and unique ways. Our church building has transformed into an ever-changing space to wonder, dream, and ponder how God is calling us to become the best versions of the people God created us to be.

The same thing has happened within our music ministry. Because of our openness and invitation to the arts community, we've had an influx of musicians join us as well. These musicians have become a part of the community largely because we sought to invite them to experience the grace of God by writing and composing new music focused on God. The result has been a beautiful worship collective filled with volunteer musicians who are constantly writing and creating worship hymns brought forth like the Psalms from the groans of our community. We now sing songs in worship each week that are authentic to our community's laments, joys, and pains.

It is amazing to think how these artists and musicians now lead our congregation in worship. They have forged a renewed understanding of what it means to glorify God by sharing everything they've been given. This collective community of not just musicians, but artists, innovators, and authors now goes by the name of Glory Revival, and they are striving to continue sharing the gifts they've been given to glorify God, to the end that we might experience a worship revival in cities all across the nation, and it all started with the power of words reaching out like arms to meet and invite.

The Misfit Mission is a collective community comprised of a whole bunch of people, trivia fans and skeptics, artists and musicians, young and old. It's something that God invites all of us to become a part of. It's a community filled with a variety of gifts and affinities, but one Spirit and one mission. It's a movement where everyone is called to bump into one another, to speak and be a word that brings forth light and life to the world around us to the extent that it encourages and inspires others to do the same.

Discussion Questions

1. What words do you use to share your experience of God with the world around you?

2. Our lives are the only scripture that most people will ever read. What does your life communicate about the grace of Jesus Christ?

3. How do you approach your mission field in ways that invite conversation, reflection, and relationships?

1. Adam Hamilton, *Seeing Gray in a World of Black and White* (Nashville: Abingdon Press, 2012); Timothy Keller, *The Reason for God in an Age of Skepticism* (New York: Riverhead Books, 2009).

CHAPTER NINE

TELLING YOUR STORY

Six years into this journey, after we've grown in our practice, size, and scope, I can now share that one of my favorite times of the week now happens to be after our weekly worship services. This is most often the time when I typically get to hear some of the best stories I have ever heard. As a pastor, people will come up to me and share their life stories. I've heard stories of coincidence, transformation, redemption, and I've even heard a few miracle stories. These are the moments I cherish the most about my Misfit Mission: hearing others' stories. There's nothing quite like the power of a great story.

One of my favorite books is a book called *Storyselling*.[1] Its premise is that "you don't sell product, you sell stories," and the best way to build a book of business is to tell stories. If you can learn to tell a good story that incorporates your product, you'll improve your sales exponentially. In fact, the authors guarantee it. The conclusion of that book was that a good story was worth its weight in gold, but I'm not so sure that increased sales makes telling a story any good.

What does make a story good? Is it an increase in sales numbers?

Inside the pages of the scripture are some the best stories you could ever read, not because of their sales or their ability to get you out of trouble (though the Bible is an all-time bestseller and I believe it will help you walk the straight and narrow), but because they lead us into a renewed understanding of who God is and who God calls us to be. This is the gospel truth.

The word *gospel* comes from the Greek word *euangelion*, which when broken down literally means "good message" or "good story" (*eu* = good, *angelion* = message) and it's from this same Greek word *euangelion* that we derive words like *evangelism* or *evangelist*, which refer to the practice of good storytelling or good storytellers. We see this word, or one of its derivatives, approximately forty-one times throughout the Bible.

As God's Misfits, we are called to be evangelists to the end that we might change the world through our stories.

In his letter to the Ephesians, the Apostle Paul wrote about how God gives us a variety of gifts so that we might employ them to change the world. He uses this word, *euangelion*, in describing one of these gifts.

> He gave some apostles, some prophets, some evangelists, and some pastors and teachers. His purpose was to equip God's people for the work of serving and building up the body of Christ until we all reach the unity of faith and knowledge of God's Son. (Eph 4:11-13)

Telling good stories and sharing the good news—the practice of evangelism—is one of the primary ways God calls us to live fully. As God's Misfits, or evangels, we are called to share the story of Jesus so that others might meet God and, in turn, discover who God created them to be.

John Wesley talked at length about our call to evangelism, and the importance of spreading and sharing the gospel with everyone we meet. He often said that the role of a great preacher and of any disciple for that matter was to have an "evangelistic" love of God and neighbor. Wesley contended that we should set ourselves on fire with the power of the Holy Spirit; in other words, we should become so enthusiastic in the faith stories we tell that people from all ends of the earth would come simply to watch us burn with the love of God. Our words matter, but the stories we tell and how we tell them matter immeasurably as well.

In Luke 14, Jesus tells a parable about a man who clearly has access to the kingdom of heaven. This man has great faith and desperately wants to share it with everyone he can. God has called him and equipped him, and the man is ready to respond. He decides to prepare a great meal, a wonderful feast, and his plan is to invite people to join him for supper.

This story precedes "the lost parables" (the lost sheep, lost coin, and prodigal son in Luke 15), a series of stories that describe the heart of God, whose love reaches out and searches for the least, the lost, the stray, the missing, and uninvited, and it comes right after Jesus's instructions for how best to display humility and hospitality in the presence of guests and first-time visitors.

In between these two types of stories, we get this story about this man who is called by God and eagerly longs to invite and introduce as many people as possible to an experience of God's forever love. This how Luke retells the story:

A certain man hosted a large dinner and invited many people. When it was time for the dinner to begin, he sent his servant to tell the invited guests, "Come! The dinner is now ready." One by one, they all began to make excuses. The first one told him, "I bought a farm and must go and see it. Please excuse me." Another said, "I bought five teams of oxen, and I'm going to check on them. Please excuse me." Another said, "I just got married, so I can't come." (Luke 14:16-20)

This man sends out all sorts of invitations, but rather than running to join him for supper, nobody comes; in fact, they run the other way. Sure, some people sent in their regrets, but most people didn't even do that. They simply ignored the invite.

The slave eventually reports the lackluster response back to the man, saying, "Nobody's coming." The man is enraged. "Why on earth aren't they coming? Don't they know what they're missing? This is going to be a great dinner. I can't let all this food go to waste . . . it's just too good." So the man commands his slave to go back out into the community to bring in all the poor, the crippled, the blind, and the lame, or as I like to call them, the wrong people—God's Misfits.

"I'll share this feast with them," he thinks.

So the slave goes and invites them, and they all come willingly and thankfully, but even after welcoming all of these folks, the slave returns to the man saying, "Master, your instructions have been followed and there is still room" (14:22). The man replies,

Go out into the roads and lanes, and *compel* the people to come in, so that my house may be filled. (Luke 14:23 NRSV)

Go out into the streets and compel people to come in.

What does it mean to compel someone?

Compelling someone requires more than an e-vite, post-card, or a general assumption that people will be interested. Compelling someone requires a connection. It requires a relationship, some familiarity, persistence, purpose, and passion. It requires being committed to doing whatever it takes, wherever people are, no matter what.

As God's Misfits, our task is to live lives that compel people to come, hear, and know the story of Jesus and his love for us. This is evangelism, this is compelling, but it begins with connection, or, in other words, listening to and learning the life stories of those around you and then, and only then, sharing our own.

Within a couple of years of launching Resurrection Downtown, we began sending teams of people outside of the walls of our church and into the world with a focus on serving and loving others the way that God first loves us. We sent teams of people internationally and domestically on mission trips, but one of my favorite trips was our first mission trip into the Appalachian Mountains. I loved hearing the transformational stories of people who went on these trips, as well as the stories of the people we encountered in those places. One of my favorite stories involved a woman named Brenda. I met Brenda while leading a team that had been commissioned to work on Brenda's roof and chimney.

Brenda's house was a quaint singlewide trailer tucked into steep hollers of Kentucky filled with lush and green kudzu. Brenda's roof was in total disrepair and so our job was to replace the entire thing, which also included several major repairs to her chimney. Throughout the week, as we worked on Brenda's roof, we knew she was there, but we never heard from her or saw her. Brenda liked to keep to herself. But we discovered that she liked to listen to us joke around with one another as we worked. On the fourth day of our weeklong trip, our work finally took us inside her house. We descended into the dark and damp house. Once inside, it didn't take too long before Brenda realized that we were going to be with her for a while. So, she attempted to open up a bit by interjecting here and there with little quips and tidbits.

At one point, she overheard one of our team members refer to me as "Pastor Scott." We noticed that this reference caused Brenda to laugh audibly. We couldn't help but look at her and wonder what was going on in her head. This was the first sign of any emotion. We couldn't understand why she would be laughing at such a simple thing. So I asked her, "What's so funny, Brenda?"

She looked back at me, still chuckling. "Well, he just called you Pastor Scott."

Brenda had originally assumed that one of the older members on our team was the pastor. There was no possible way in her mind that I, barely thirty years old, could have been the pastor. Clearly, I was unlike any pastor she had ever seen before, so she laughed. She thought they were teasing me.

It took us awhile, but eventually our team convinced her that I was indeed the pastor, and when that happened, we noticed her demeanor change again. She got really quiet; in fact, she went away and hid.

So, back to work we went. We worked for another four hours without seeing Brenda. It wasn't until we were preparing to leave that Brenda decided to reappear and re-engage the group.

We were packing up and she approached me directly. "What kind of pastor are you?"

"United Methodist," I answered.

She inquired, "How is that different than a Baptist pastor?"

"Well, there are some differences, I suppose...but why do you ask?"

Then it happened. Brenda shared her story.

"Eight years ago today, I lost my eleven-year-old son in a car accident. He was hit by a drunk driver while walking alongside the road. The driver of the car was fifteen years old. He received thirty days detention in juvenile hall. I see him whenever I'm out and about in the town's stores, but that's not all. You see, when I went to my son's funeral, two of my preachers told me that my son didn't make it to heaven. They said he hadn't claimed Jesus Christ as his own personal savior. Then they told me, at his funeral, that I needed to stop worrying about him and begin worrying about my own salvation...because once I make it to heaven, I won't ever worry about anything ever again."

As she shared this story with me, others were listening in and we all found ourselves fighting back the tears. I had all sorts of questions going through my head. I thought, "Who on earth would have told her that? And what's wrong with those people?" And then I found myself thinking, "Here is this broken woman, someone who had been cast out into the margins. She was a misfit by all accounts in her community, and now after all that, she was sharing her story with us for the first time in over eight years. What could we say? What could we do? How could we free her from the shackles of the story she had been sold by those other two pastors?"

We were paralyzed. There was nothing we could do. So we listened. We sat next to her in her grief and mourning, beside the memories of her deceased son, and the debilitating pain that had been following her for eight long and arduous years.

We were with her for quite awhile. It was quiet at times, but then we couldn't help but share our stories detailing the nature of God's perfect love. We talked about Jesus's birth, his life, his words, his death, his resurrection, and the love that persisted throughout it all, a love that will not let us go.

Then we began to simply share our own stories, describing how each of our lives had been transformed and were continuing to be changed by God's forgiveness, mercy, and grace. We shared about how our faith in God made us better versions of the people we were created to be. I shared that I considered myself to be a better husband, friend, son, and brother because of my faith in God and God's unconditional love for me. I sought to love others as well as myself, the same way as God first loved me. I also shared how my faith in God allows me to have hope always, knowing like Paul that the there is nothing I could ever do or leave undone that could separate me from the love of God (cf. Rom 8:38-39). Finally, after all of that, I couldn't help but tell her that the story her two pastors tried to sell her in the midst of her grief (urging her to forget her son because he was lost and would never be found) wasn't true. Jesus loves us and never leaves us, but instead pursues us and goes with us even to the end of the age, and because of that we can always have hope.

We didn't have all the right words to say, but because we listened to Brenda, and then after listening to her had the courage to share our stories, she broke out in tears. Through the sharing of stories, Brenda's life opened up and so did ours. Our hearts broke open right along with hers, and light pierced the surrounding darkness as together we became one in the love of Christ as we embraced. Sweaty, stinky, strangers hugged it out in the middle of Appalachia.

We left a few days later, and a few weeks after that we received word from the directors of the mission. They shared with us that Brenda had encountered an unexpected word of hope from what must have been a choir of angels. They said that ever since we had left, she had been smiling, something she hadn't been able to do for quite some time. Unbeknownst to us, Brenda had been withering inside for eight years.

Looking back on that trip, we were so fortunate to stumble across her path. When the time came, we accepted her invitation to listen to her story, and then we shared ours. She emptied herself of all that had been shackling and plaguing her, and then by emptying ourselves in response, God was able to fill both her and us with God's perfect love.

This is the power of sharing stories. This is the power of the gospel. This is what it looks like to do the things that God does. This is what it looks like to compel someone to join you on the Misfit Mission. It starts with listening and continues when you're bold enough to share your story authentically and courageously in return.

Compelling people to act involves listening, radical hospitality, and authentic humility, and it almost always involves strangers or neighbors. It requires that you constantly attune your heads and hearts to those around you and then reach out to them sacrificially the way that Christ reaches out to us.

In the Gospel of John, Jesus tells his disciples,

> I give you a new commandment: Love each other. Just as I have loved you, so you also must love each other. This is how everyone will know that you are my disciples, when you love each other. (John 13:34-35)

"Just as I have loved you," he says, "you are to love one another." How did Jesus love us? By sharing everything he had with us to the point that he was broken open and poured out for us.

As he was dying on the cross, he listened to the voices of the people standing in the crowd. They were sharing their stories of insult. Yelling out things like "Crucify him! He saved others, why can't he save himself?" (cf. Matt 27:42). Jesus listened first and then, as people emptied their verbal insults from these deep reservoirs of pain and suffering, Jesus cried out with everything he had. He shared his story, saying, "Father, forgive them, for they don't know what they're doing" (Luke 23:34). He literally shared everything he had—all of his love, mercy, and forgiveness—to the end that we might be filled. That we might go, live, and do likewise.

In order live fully, in order to go and do likewise, we need to set aside the prevailing thought that we can't or shouldn't share with others all that we have. We are called to love as

Christ first loved us, which means we must love others by sharing everything we have and, in order to do this, we must be willing to share who we really are, what we're really going through, or what is holding us back, weighing us down, or plaguing us. We must share who we are.

I love the psalmist who writes,

> Come close and listen, all you who honor God; I will tell you what God has done for me: My mouth cried out to him with praise on my tongue. If I had cherished evil in my heart, my Lord would not have listened. But God definitely listened. He heard the sound of my prayer. Bless God! He didn't reject my prayer; he didn't withhold his faithful love from me. (Ps 66:16-20)

The psalmist boldly proclaims, "Come, all you who fear. Come, all who are shackled. Come, all you who are in the darkness, for I will not be quiet, I will not be silent anymore. Let me tell you what the Lord has done for me. Even in my anger, God did not reject me, but God's steadfast love remained with me. God loves me and will never let me go. Not even my anger excludes me from feasting at the table, nor will my questions or my doubt, or my addiction, or my whatever..."

Living into the Misfit Mission requires that we are willing to share our stories with others and listen to those who share theirs. Then trust that by sharing the story of your life in Christ, others will be transformed.

At Resurrection Downtown, this kind of radical vulnerability or authenticity pervades our band of misfits. People are who they are. They don't hide from one another or the burdens they are carrying, but instead share vulnerably and courageously with the people around them. Perhaps this is the case because there are so many babies being born downtown. In the past five years, in our church community, there have been stretches where we have averaged two or three babies born per week. With that comes a lot of visible joy and excitement, but also a certain level of vulnerability. Everywhere you turn there are babies crying, spitting up, or running around shouting, which means nobody can pretend as though they have it all together because everyone is simply trying to survive. However, even in this vulnerable community, one byproduct of this baby boom has been an increased reluctance to want to share anything that is less than joyful when it comes to having babies. People don't like talking about things like miscarriages, depression, or birth defects, even though these things are happening all of the time too.

Luana started attending Resurrection Downtown during one of our more intense baby booms, and, sure enough, upon meeting her, she shared that she was expecting a baby boy. Luana and her husband quickly joined the church and got connected to the life of our community. They were happy and healthy, and yet the whole time something was stirring.

About a month after her baby was born, Luana wrote me a letter:

> I gave birth to my beautiful son in February of 2012. Little did I know the darkest days of my life would soon follow. I felt great the first week after delivery and proud at how well I was handling a newborn. Then something changed. Three weeks after delivery, I began experiencing a profound fatigue. I thought that was normal since I was sleep deprived dealing with a colicky baby. My condition quickly turned to anxiety and DEEP sadness. I didn't want to get out of bed, I just felt like crying. Shame, guilt and anger took over my life. I wanted to disappear.

My symptoms worsened with my mom's departure. I was convinced I was a bad mother and a terrible wife. Beginning in June, my symptoms worsened to the point that I began having suicidal thoughts and had even formulated a few plans. I laid up in bed and wondered what my family's life would be like without me. I was of no use to them in this condition. I just laid there paralyzed with fear, paralyzed to the point that I could not act on the suicidal thoughts. By the grace of God, I made it until morning. Sunday morning. God sustained me through the night.

Throughout her private battle with postpartum depression, Luana and her husband attended church as usual. She did not tell anyone about her suicidal thoughts. She was scared to tell anyone. She couldn't focus on anything during the service, so she just cried and cried. She prayed that God would rescue her from this overwhelming darkness. Then something compelled her to share her story.

In a flash of courage, she told her husband. He listened first and then he hugged his wife. Moments later they called me. As they shared their story over the phone, I listened to them. Then I prayed with them and immediately shared their story with a counselor. A few days after that, Luana was admitted into an outpatient program where she stayed for six weeks. While there, she learned a great deal of personal skills, but before any of those practical measures, she learned firsthand that God is good and God is faithful all the time. She learned that even when we walk through the darkness, God is there with us because God loves us and never lets us go. She learned that in the midst of chaos, God continues to offer us a story of hope and peace through the sharing of stories. Most importantly, she learned that God loves us despite our faults, fears, and failures, and she learned all of this because of the ways that people listened to her as she shared her story with them, and then how they shared their stories of the love of Christ in return through connection and community.

What has followed since has been a miraculous story of healing and renewal. As I look back on it now, I can see God's hand on every page.

A few months later, Luana asked if I might be willing to baptize her son. As I stood there in the center of the sanctuary, I couldn't help but think back to that time when she was on the edge of despair and what would have happened if Luana didn't share her story, or if nobody had been present to listen and share theirs in return. Telling her story paved the way for new life. Exposing her pain made new life possible. This is God's Misfit Way.

Following all of this, Luana started working with young mothers. She started to find avenues to share her story with others who might not know what to do or how to break free from their guilt and shame and fear. She also made herself available to people who simply need someone to listen to their story. She wants to connect with as many people as possible to the end that others come to know of God's never-ending love for them because, after all, everyone has a place at the dinner banquet.

Luana's story, Brenda's story, all of our stories remind us that the power of our invitation comes from our testimonies and those are best shared by offering a listening ear first. Then, by sharing our own stories, by emptying ourselves in response, people will be filled by God's grace and mercy and, in turn, feel compelled to join us in experiencing renewed sense of strength that goes along with God's perfect love for us.

It's hard to share stories, it's hard to give it all away, it's hard to allow others in, and yet this is what Christ does time and time again. Jesus calls and invites us to go and do likewise.

What's your story? Have you ever broken yourself open and poured yourself out? Are you creating space for others in your life to share theirs with you? Are you listening?

We are called to share stories. We are called to be evangelists, to reach out remind friends and neighbors that this banquet is prepared for everyone, people of all types, going through all sorts of things. But the only way they'll know that—the only way they'll be compelled to respond to the invitation—is if they hear the story first.

The Misfit Mission isn't always about sharing the good news of Jesus Christ, but it's about sharing the good news of what Jesus Christ has done for you.

My hope in writing this has been to share just a portion of my experience of what the good news of Jesus Christ has done in my life through the people of Resurrection Downtown, and now my ongoing hope is that you will live forward faithfully without fear into the future that God has for you: a future filled with hope unending, love unconditional, and God's holy and surprising adventure.

Discussion Questions

1. What is your story and how is your life different because of the grace of Jesus Christ?

2. Who's story are you interested in learning? Where can you go to listen and be present in the midst of strangers?

3. What's stopping you from going there?

1. Scott West and Mitch Anthony, *Storyselling for Financial Advisors: How Top Producers Sell* (Fort Lauderdale, FL: Kaplan Publishing, 2000).

CPSIA information can be obtained
at www.ICGtesting.com
Printed in the USA
LVOW04s2330290116

472928LV00003B/3/P